You

Can Be

God's Agent →

for

Change

CATALYSTS

handwritten inscription: A catalyst to the Kingdom of God.

You
Can Be
God's Agent

CATALYSTS

for

Change

BEV MURRILL

© Copyright 2007 - Bev Murrill

All rights reserved. This book is protected under the copyright laws. This book may not be copied or reprinted for commercial gain or profit. The use of short quotations or occasional page copying for personal or group study is permitted and encouraged. Permission will be granted upon request. Unless otherwise identified, Scripture quotations are taken from the New Living Translation, copyright 1996. Used by permission of Tyndale House Publishers, Inc. Wheaton, Illinois 60189. All Rights Reserved. Scripture quotations marked AMP are taken from the Amplified® Bible, Copyright © 1954, 1958, 1962, 1964, 1965, 1987 by The Lockman Foundation. Used by permission. All Rights Reserved. Scripture quotations marked NIV are taken from the Holy Bible, New International Version®. Copyright © 1973, 1978, 1984 by International Bible Society. Used by permission of Zondervan Publishing House. All rights reserved. Scripture quotations marked NASB are taken from the New American Standard Bible®, Copyright 1960, 1962, 1963, 1968, 1971, 1972, 1973, 1975, 1977, 1995 by The Lockman Foundation. Used by permission. All rights reserved. Scripture quotations marked KJV are taken from the King James Version of the Bible. Scripture quotations marked NKJV are taken from the New King James Version. Copyright © 1982 by Thomas Nelson, Inc. Used by permission. All rights reserved. Please note that Destiny Image Europe's publishing style capitalizes certain pronouns in Scripture that refer to the Father, Son, and Holy Spirit, and may differ from some Bible publishers' styles.

Take note that the name satan and related names are not capitalized. We choose not to acknowledge him, even to the point of violating grammatical rules.

DESTINY IMAGE EUROPE™ **srl**
Via Maiella, 1
66020 San Giovanni Teatino (Ch) - Italy

"Changing the world, one book at a time."

This book and all other Destiny Image Europe™ books are available at Christian bookstores and distributors worldwide.

To order products, or for any other correspondence:

DESTINY IMAGE EUROPE™ **srl**
Via Acquacorrente, 6
65123 - Pescara - Italy
Tel. +39 085 4716623 - Fax: +39 085 4716622
E-mail: info@eurodestinyimage.com

Or reach us on the Internet: **www.eurodestinyimage.com**

ISBN 13: 978-88-89127-44-5

For Worldwide Distribution, Printed in Italy.

1 2 3 4 5 6 7 8/10 09 08 07

Dedication

To the God who owns the "catalysts" on a thousand hills (see Ps. 50:10)—thank You for changing my life forever and for never giving up on the task of making me more like You.

To my husband of 35 years, Rick—you are the most faithful and loving friend I've ever had, and the single most stabilizing force in my life outside of the Word of God.

To my children—Dan and Ondine, Skye and Matt, Toby and Katie, Seth and Sherelle—I will never produce anything as valuable as you are...and you only ever increase in value. I'm grateful to God for each one of you and am more proud of you than words can express. Thank you for forgiving me when I have been less than you deserve and for loving me always and unconditionally.

To my darling granddaughters—Meekah Angel, Caelan Amber, Echo Jazmine Tobin—you delight my heart, and I pray that God will cause you to grow strong in Him and in the power of His might, enriching the world around you with His grace, joy, and love.

With deep thanks to my dear mum, Dorothy Bunyan, who died before this book was released, for the legacy of courage and optimism she left me.

Acknowledgments

It is with deep appreciation that I acknowledge all the dear people I have worked with over the years I have served as a leader in that most beautiful of all institutions—the Church of Jesus Christ. I am so thankful to all of those who have stood with me in love and patience, in season and out of season. Though the years and the plans of God have caused us to take different paths, so many people have encouraged me to go on in His purposes.

Most particularly I acknowledge and appreciate the two churches Rick and I have pastored, and the people who have served with us there:

∼ Highlands Christian Church, Mittagong, Australia.

∼ Christian Growth Centre, Chelmsford, England.

Thank you for all you have taught me and the growth I have sustained through the precious time I have spent in these two wonderful congregations. Through you I have learned the value of repentance and forgiveness, along with the grace of God, without which none of us can live.

Endorsements

I find Bev's teaching inspirational and profound. That's not simply because she has some good ideas from God, or because she is able to articulate those ideas in a coherent and interesting presentation; but it is because Bev is also an excellent wordsmith. She is a craftswoman, who somehow manages to take biblical truth and prophetic inspiration and let these things shape and be shaped by the very words that are chosen to deliver them—which results in poetry, whose rhythm and accent carries ideas through mind and heart into the spirit of who we are. I am really excited, then, that such poetic gifting can now move the reader as well as the listener.

Martin Young
Senior Minister
Rising Brook Baptist Church
Stafford, United Kingdom

This is not just another book on leadership; this is about a leadership revolution that has its beginnings with Jesus. Bev Murrill takes experience and revelation and effectively communicates what we all need to hear. For we live in a time where the words, "If we always do what we have always done, we will get what we have always got" could never be truer. Bev, together with her husband, Rick, have lived this for many years, challenging the way things have been done in order for them and others to embrace the "new things" that God has for us. Bev will challenge, inspire, and teach you how to embrace something that can change generations. After al,l we do become transformed when we make new the way we have been thinking; and to do this, you need to receive *new* information. Here it is!

Mark Crawford
National Leader
Bethesda Ministries International (BMI)
Australia

Catalysts by Bev Murrill presents an insightful and hard hitting challenge to the kind of personal purity and obedience that transforms Christian leaders and consequently their ministry. As an established and mature leadership practitioner, Murrill, with deep conviction and the wisdom that comes from years in ministry, addresses the everyday challenges of life, with the inspiration of the Holy Spirit. Digesting and responding to this book might just change your life!

Ron Hannaford
Director of Distance Learning
Fuller Theological Seminary
Pasadena, CA
USA

There is a new generation of leaders whom God is preparing in our day. They might not yet be well-known in the eyes of the world, but they are known by God. Prepared in obscurity through the dealings of God, they place more value in character than in charisma alone. These are the chosen ones, the world changers that this book is calling out to. I have known Bev Murrill and her husband, Rick, for many years. They are, in my opinion, truly great leaders in Christ's Church who have borne much fruit for the Kingdom. This book has been birthed out of the dealings of God throughout their own amazing journey and will impact you to your core. As I read this book, there were times when I had to put it down and let God deal with my heart before I could continue. I am sure that it will affect you in just the same way.

David Palmer
Senior Pastor
Pine Rivers Assembly of God Church
Queensland, Australia

Bev Murrill has written this book straight from her heart. She has been and still is a catalyst for godly change in the Body of Christ and in the community she serves. Like all people who pioneer change, she has sacrificed comfort in some areas, and endured and worked her way through pain in others, all because she sees a bigger picture. She sees a Church and a society transformed by God's power, and she desires to be a part of what God is doing in the earth today. This book is itself a powerful catalyst for change and influence. I encourage all current leaders and also those who aspire to leadership to not only read it, but to embrace its principles. It will also provide keys for those who might not regard themselves as leaders, but who desire to change their world. It is a book of great depth, yet very readable, and there is Holy Spirit-breathed life in its pages. It is written out of a wealth of experience but also through direct revelation; it is a must-read for all those who desire to become everything that

God would have them be and everyone who longs to be a part of the answer for the Church and the world.

Sheena Ryan
Staff Pastor/Itinerant Minister
Suncoast Christian Church
Queensland, Australia

Bev has been a great inspiration and provocation to me. She is a woman who is not willing to settle for mediocrity but has a passion to see people released into being the best expression that God has created them to be. She definitely has something to say to the Church today.

Lynn Swart
Worship Pastor
Southampton Community Church
Southampton, United Kingdom

Bev is no "ivory tower" academic, writing from a distant place. She writes from a life consumed with a passion to be the message, to influence and not be influenced, to pioneer rather than settle. Over the years I have known Bev, I have seen that her desire to raise up leaders and equip the Church works in real life. Having decided what she is prepared to die for, Bev has defined who she will live for. This comes across in this no-holds-barred, fast-paced book on what it means to be a catalyst in this generation and the generations to come. If a catalyst agitates—get ready to be challenged.

Paul Gutteridge
Senior Pastor
Christian Growth Centre
Chelmsford, United Kingdom

"In order to be a change agent for the Kingdom, the catalyst must first be permanently and continuously changed by God, which isn't as easy to do as it is to say." As Bev Murrill encourages us to pursue God's purpose in this world, it soon becomes clear that, from use of Scripture and personal experience, Bev has come back with an inextinguishable conviction to walk a path that many have failed to navigate successfully and which even fewer have humbly returned to tread again alongside those still walking or stumbling, wherever we are. Don't miss out.

Paul Adlington
Senior Pastor
The Bear Church
London, United Kingdom

Bev Murrill has written a book that brings a fresh look and insight to the whole perspective of Kingdom leadership for today. Bev has also written in a manner that dynamically opens up the pages of the Bible and is at the same time practical, interesting, and challenging. She has a style that conveys her heart, and it's just as if she is in the same room personally chatting and encouraging you in your discipleship and leadership development. I would highly recommend the book especially as a tool for practical insight as well as for its simple yet insightful ways in enabling today's individuals to grow in the wisdom, grace, and power of the Kingdom of God.

Kevin Potter
Pastor
Church of God International (CGI)

Table of Contents

Foreword by Mark Kelsey

This book is both inspiring and challenging. As I worked through its pages, I found myself being inspired by the simple call to live in and give my life to the purpose of God. As I kept reading, a powerful realization hit me: To do this is going to require everything I have and everything I am! I was increasingly challenged as I realized that to stay on track, I have to maintain a focus and dedication to ensure my life is a worthy example of living in God.

I love reading a book that is formed out of a life of a real person—someone who has experienced all that life has to throw at it and can continue to pursue God in the midst of challenge. I remember the first time I heard Bev speak at a leadership conference, which she and her husband, Rick, hosted in the UK. They were not only pastoring and building a significant church in that nation, planting churches throughout the UK and beyond, but also wanting to equip other men and women to do the same. Their heart for people and their love for the house of God and for the ministry were acutely evident. As Bev began to preach, I was immediately impressed by her realness and her insight into the Word of God but became increasingly aware that this was more than a message "prepared" for a conference, but was an impassioned and experienced appeal for believers to discover the person who He had called them to be. She was not trying to impress but to transform the listeners. That passion feeds its way all through this book.

Probably one of the most misunderstood concepts is the notion called, "the purpose of God." Believers through the ages have wondered what the purpose of God is, how it gets accomplished, and how their life relates to it. Of course, to the well initiated, it becomes very clear after a while that our lives and the purpose of God cannot be separated. In fact, our lives, the way we live them, and the extent to which we allow God to use them is what the purpose of God is all about. This book helps the reader see this more clearly.

Life is a series of choices that in the end determine the direction we set our lives towards. We have the power to align or misalign our lives with God and what He is attempting to accomplish through us. The idea of a new generation is not so much about a new group of young people but about a new way of thinking or at least a different way of thinking—different to the patterns of the world and different to the self-focused, individualistic trends that currently dominate our cultures. This is a generation that is servant-hearted at its core, focused outward and toward God, that is willing to do what it needs to do in order to be a catalyst for change, a catalyst for the purposes of God on the earth. It is certainly not a generation of the fainthearted, for as humble and insignificant as they might seem to the untrained eye, they are the true heroes and warriors who pursue a greater and more noble pursuit beyond their own immediate desires.

Most people have dreams at the beginning. They attack life with the zest of vision and desire for significance. Early in our pursuits, opposition comes. The ability to see beyond the obstacle or even more profoundly to see within the obstacle what lies hidden is a rare gift indeed. Because it is in the prison that the dream will begin to be fulfilled, beginning with the dream of change of our own lives. There are not two paths, but only one. There are, however, two purposes. We choose which purpose we will follow and which outcome we will arrive at. Bev shows us in this book how things that happen to us cannot cause us to fail and miss the purpose of God, but in fact, it is in these things that we are changed and we can then become an agent of change for others.

The common pitfalls of modern man—the struggle with self-image, the temptation to live as a victim, the habit of feeding our lives with all the wrong input, and tendency to value life on its external merits only—are all profoundly addressed by Bev. And our thinking soon becomes redirected so that these issues are seen with a new perspective...one that clears the way for change, life, and freedom.

Read this book with your weight on your front foot...ready for change, ready for challenge, and ready to get free! Enjoy!

Mark Kelsey
Assistant Senior Minister
Christian City Church, Oxford Falls, Australia

Foreword by Mal Fletcher

Influence—it's a hot topic of discussion in today's Church.

Many voices urge us as Christians to arise and engage the culture of our times. They call us to do more than maintain the status quo—to pioneer a new way forward. However, very few voices emerge to show us how that's done!

Bev Murrill is an exception to that rule.

In 25 years of travelling the world, speaking to audiences of all races and ages, I've discovered that influence is not a product of our celebration of the past, or our enjoyment of the present. Long-lasting, society-changing influence is a direct result of how much we engage the future.

John F. Kennedy said that those who look only to the past or the present are certain to miss the future.

For so many people in our society, the church is anachronistic—an out-of-date organization with little to offer post-modern thinking. In this view, the church is not a thriving community of people empowered for life; the church is a building where people go to listen to songs nobody wants to sing and sermons nobody wants to hear. The only people who enjoy church are those who have nothing more exciting to live for; they find solace in the comforts of the past because they see no light of hope in their future.

Nothing could be further from the truth! Christians are divinely empowered to be the most hopeful and forward-looking people on the planet. After all, we serve a future-minded Lord. Throughout His earthly ministry, He constantly looked to tomorrow. Never once did Jesus indulge in wistful nostalgia. Even in the face of imminent death by crucifixion, He remained fixed on the "joy still in the future" (see Heb. 12:2).

Bev Murrill believes that the Church can and should enter a new season of influence in society. In the very first chapter of this book, she makes a profound observation. "The relevance of the past," she writes, "only has power to the degree in which it is used as a building block to construct the future."

A new season of influence, she says, requires that Christians add to their heritage a fresh sense of where God is taking the Church and the culture next. Bev traces a line from our past into our God-ordained future. Drawing from the examples of our biblical forebears, she identifies timeless principles of influence and applies them with prophetic skill to today's situations and needs. In particular, she shows us what the leaders of this new era of influence will look like.

The book you hold in your hands is much more than another reflection on where the Church is today. It is a passionate cry for the Church to become something more—it is a rallying call into our prophetic future.

Bev writes lucidly, with an engaging and thought-provoking style. Her compassion for the seekers in our world—those yet to find hope in Christ—is matched by her passion for fellow Christians, whom she sets out to inspire and equip for greater holiness, faith, vision, and ultimately, influence.

Influence is born of insight. The chapters you're about to read will give you insight—into your world, your life, and your future as they are seen from God's perspective. If you're ready to influence your world more than it impacts you, if you're ready to leave huge footprints in the sands of time and invest your life in something that will outlive you, read on...

Mal Fletcher
Founder Next Wave International
And Edges TV
London 2006

Preface

THE PURPOSE OF A CATALYST...

A catalyst is a tiny agent for change which, when introduced to a situation or chemical compound, irrevocably changes the compound or situation without itself being changed. The introduction of a catalyst not only often causes heat but also a speeding up of the molecular structure of the situation to which it is applied. When Christians operate as catalysts for the purposes of God, the results are life changing.

Christians are called as catalysts to change their world without being corrupted by it. Introduced into any situation, be it work or your neighborhood or even a church, we can become the missing element that transforms an inert or even deadly situation into an amazing opportunity for people to meet with Jesus firsthand and be changed forever by the encounter.

Before we can operate as God's change agents, however, we must first be changed ourselves, and it is for that purpose this book is written, with the firm belief that when God is allowed to work continually to change our hearts, He can use us to change our world!

Bev Murrill
A tiny catalyst for a great God

Introduction

The Christ of the New Testament produced a people whose faith compelled them to risk everything to live for God, and as a consequence the world was turned upside down. In the ensuing centuries, however, this type of faith became increasingly rare as the Church increased in respectability becoming more socially acceptable. There were, however, exceptional pockets of deep faith in every nation that continued to breed Christians determined to live their lives for the purpose of bringing freedom to their world. These people invaded regions where the power of darkness ruled, and brought the light of Jesus Christ in amazing ways. This type of faith stands in stark juxtaposition, however, to conservative Christianity that represents to society nothing but pomp and ceremony, lists of rules, infighting, self-aggrandizement, and political correctness gone mad. Increasing impotence has weakened the message of the Church, rendering it pale, stale, and too frail to make any difference to the world it has been called to influence.

However, God has no Plan B. It has been said that the Church is the only institution that exists for the benefit of its non-members. God's decision to use the Church as a catalyst to change the world is as unwavering now as it was when He first commissioned that small and disparate group of followers. God doesn't use armies to change nations; He uses disciples. He still catches the attention of individuals at their own burning bush and persuades them to go with Him to alter the course of history, because the answer to transforming nations lies in those who themselves have been transformed by His grace.

Ineffectual Christianity breeds emasculated churches filled with people who are dissatisfied with their faith and suffering massive guilt because of it. Courage and purpose from the heart of God must be injected directly into our hearts if we are to see this situation change. Jesus is the Catalyst to change our lives, and He calls us to emulate Him in this for the sake of the world He loves. Called to usher in the Kingdom of God, Christians are the only people with any answer to the problem of sin and sickness that intimidates and overwhelms every person, every suburb, and every nation.

A catalyst precipitates change without itself being permanently changed, and every implementation of change always requires the introduction of a catalyst, the size of which is immaterial. Jesus operated as the most powerful catalyst for the purposes of God; His life changed the world and brought the Kingdom of Heaven to earth. He calls us to do the same—the Church reincarnating His presence in every street, town, and city across the globe.

However, to usher in the Kingdom takes more than a decision to do so. In order to be a change agent for the Kingdom, the catalyst itself must first be permanently and continuously changed by God, which isn't as easy to do as it is to say. It entails the willingness to embrace much personal pain as hidden issues surface to be challenged by the grace of God. Long held misunderstandings and deep resentments demand our attention, as He in turn demands from us a Christlikeness that can come only through dying to self and being renewed in His likeness. Issues relating to honesty and faithfulness, truth and self-sacrifice come head-to-head with our longing to hide and be comfortable and have something for ourselves. We long for freedom, but we are lured by the seduction of sin into bondage. All these things wrestle together in the life of every Christian as the battle rages over who will have the right to rule our life.

And while the battle rages, creation groans and travails, waiting in desperation for the revealing of the children of God (see Rom. 8:18-22). Only as God's people stand up to be who He has called us to be will creation receive the answers it is so desperate for—answers that lie in Christians alone. Who else but the people of God can introduce the love and truth of Jesus Christ into the world, yet it all depends on our willingness to be changed into His image. When Christians are willing to be changed by the power of God, their world will automatically follow suit.

CHAPTER ONE

A New Generation

...all I hear every day is people crying out for a savior.

Clark Kent—aka Superman

In the movie, *Superman Returns*, Clark Kent comes back to Metropolis after a long time away, and one of the first things he sees as he walks into the pressroom of the *Daily Planet* is an old newspaper article written by Lois Lane. The headline reads, "Why the World Doesn't Need Superman." During their conversation, he says to her, "That's strange, because all I hear every day is people crying out for a savior."

Movies always reflect the current mood of society, and the comment made by Clark incisively pinpoints the mood of the 21st century. The world is desperate for a Savior, whether they know it or not. It's this desperation that drives the terrorists as

The days of dreaming about what used to be have come to an end; the relevance of the past has power only to the degree in which it is used as a building block to construct the future.

much as those whom they terrorize. Deep in the heart of humankind is an unquenchable longing for relationship with an unknown God who cares enough to come to our rescue.

The key to Jesus' victory as Savior of the world lies not in His overwhelming power but in His willingness to lay it aside to become one of us. He associated with those He came to save in an act of identificational surrender which has no comparison. To understand the depth of sacrifice that came with this act is impossible. All we know is that He made a choice to put aside all that made Him God, in order to become all that would make him human. In doing this, He personified all that humankind is and ever could be—a selfless incarnation enabling Him to use His power to bring freedom to multiple generations.

IDENTIFICATION

Only those who can identify with a society can influence it. The world as we know it is changing radically, and in almost every nation and culture, life as it is lived in the 21st century is vastly different from the experiences of previous generations. Old paradigms have been erased, leaving society by turns bewildered and confused, despairing and enraged, as it endeavors to find workable solutions to new and ancient problems. The call on the Church is to lead nations, influence governments, and bring change to countless millions whose perspective on living can ultimately be summed up in a few words—*you're born, you live, you die*—and yet who long for something more, something beyond the pointlessness of the grueling struggle to survive.

God is raising a new generation of Christians of every age and race who can relate with the world as it is now, not as it used to be. He is doing a fresh thing in the earth, and in order for the Church to work with Him effectively, it must also be renewed. The days of dreaming about what used to be have come to an end; the relevance of the past has power only to the degree in which it is used as a building block to construct the future. Every new generation requires new generation leaders; and new generation leadership is not confined to the young, nor is it confined within the walls of church structure. Its credibility is to be found in a mind-set rather than in a generational or sacred context.

The new season requires the sort of leadership that will provide the input and direction necessary to enable the Church's heritage to combine with the freshness of God's new season in order to influence tomorrow. People will always need love, acceptance, and forgiveness; but society's wrapping paper changes constantly, and the methods and paradigms of the Church must change too. Jesus is the perfect model of a new generation leader as He knew how to work within and without the walls erected by religiosity. He didn't need a title or a role in the synagogue in order to be an influencer of the people.

The message of Jesus Christ is as powerful now as it ever was. The Great Commission still commands us to proclaim the Gospel and reflect His life to a world soaked in pain and racked with confusion. For this hi-tech, hi-touch generation, it is vital that Christians engage their culture with a depth and vigor that is not only purposeful but also relatable. Relevance, when coupled with realism, has an amazing way of reaching people's hearts.

Every new generation requires new generation leaders; and new generation leadership is not confined to the young, nor is it confined within the walls of church structure.

A New Generation Leader

But Jesus called them together and said, "You know that in this world kings are tyrants, and officials lord it over the people beneath them. But among you it should be quite different. Whoever wants to be a leader among you must be your servant, and whoever wants to be first must become your slave. For even I, the Son of Man, came here not to be served but to serve others, and to give My life as a ransom for many" (Matthew 20:25-28).

Regardless of the century a person is born in, regardless of his or her nation or generation, regardless of how modern and contemporary the music and programs are, the old generation model of leadership still thrives today. Here Jesus refers to that kind of leader as He identifies the model of leadership the world uses. Yet His words encourage His disciples to abandon this old paradigm and embrace a unique and relatively unknown style of leadership—His style. He points out that the primary motivation of leaders who model the world's philosophy is to be acknowledged and valued as important. Being in charge of others is the measure of success as far as the old generation leaders are concerned; they interpret the approval of others as the mark of their leadership. They measure their own success by comparing themselves with their peers, and the personal satisfaction of their role is determined by how important they are in the eyes of others. It is very common for church and ministry leaders to embrace the old model...but that's not how Jesus led.

When Jesus spoke about leadership, His words cut across everything they ever knew or understood about leading, and it is the same for us today. His words run counter to all we have consciously or subconsciously absorbed about the role of leadership in church life. His perspective of the servant leader scrapes painfully across the veneer that has been layered over our souls not only by the enculturation of our society but also by the longing of our own hearts.

To influence a new generation demands a new way of living, of thinking, and of acting. To lead God's people His way demands a heavenly mind-set that we can't achieve on our own because it's diametrically opposed to what we really want. Our hearts are deceitful—we long to be significant and important—that's the craving of our old nature. But Jesus teaches that to lead a new generation, we must be a new generation leader and He models what that looks like. Pity the churches and communities who must endure leaders who have lost perspective on their call and are in leadership for what they can get out of it.

His perspective of the servant leader scrapes painfully across the veneer that has been layered over our souls not only by the enculturation of our society but also by the longing of our own hearts.

The crux of our capacity to serve the world in the way that Jesus did is found in our ability to be free from its influences…and therein lies the rub! Despite our best intentions, despite the determination we feel to make a difference for God, we are not aware of the degree to which the things we are opposed to in others are still resident in our own hearts and lives. Until we see ourselves clearly and truthfully and are willing to make the choices to live in transparency before God and others, our hearts will always fool us into thinking that we are free from the problems we observe in our neighbors. It's the old log-and-speck theory, where the presence of the log prevents us from realizing how little impact we can have on other people's problems. Unless and until we deal with the issues of our own hearts, we will never have the power to help others with those same issues. Whether we know it or not, we are disabled from dealing with the effects of sin in our communities, nations, and churches, by the simple fact that we have not eradicated those things from our own lives.

CHANGING THE LEADERSHIP GUARD (2 KINGS 9–10)

Judah was in a mess! The kings who had ruled it had generally gone from bad to worse, and even those who had started well continually found their effectiveness aborted by issues of fear and pride that lay undealt with in their hearts. Then God gave Elisha a strategy for the way forward, inherent in which was a changing of the leadership guard…literally, new wine and a new wine skin.

Elisha instructed one of his disciples to go and anoint a new king—a dangerous thing to do because the old king wasn't dead yet. It is remarkable how often God raises up new leaders in a time when the old generation leadership is still running the show. The current king was evil like his father before him, and Elisha's mission was to identify, raise up, and commission people who would make cleansing the land their priority.

The battle begins and ends in our own heart. If we can win it there, we will win it in every area of responsibility.

Arriving at the camp, the young messenger took his courage in both hands and approached Jehu's tent, only to find himself in the middle of a war room conference. Assembled together were the cream of the Judean army, strong young soldiers and seasoned warriors who were preparing for battle.

I have written to you who are mature because you know Christ, the one who is from the beginning. I have written to you who are young because you are strong with God's word living in your hearts, and you have won your battle with satan (1 John 2:14b).

Spiritual maturity doesn't automatically arrive with the years; it increases in a person as the character of Christ increases, developing as the young Christian takes the time to grow strong in godly principles, learning how to fight and win the issues warring within himself or herself. The optimum is for both young and old to stand together in a battle where godly mind-sets rather than muscle dictate who has strength for the fight.

The young gain maturity from consistently winning their own internal wars. The challenge for those who are older is to continue to place their reliance on the God of the supernatural rather than on their years of experience. When good kings went down in the Old Testament, it was because familiarity with their role as leader had gradually inured them to the power of God. Although they had seen God do amazing miracles early in their reign when they knew there was no way to win except through faith in God, they had become increasingly comfortable in their own positions as the years passed. When the enemy attacked again in later years, almost all of them resorted to stripping the Temple of its treasure to bribe neighboring kings to help them, rather than trust the God who had miraculously provided for them in the past. Fear, coupled with the familiarity of their role, robbed them of the faith they needed to rely on God in their time of challenge. They had lost perspective that the battle begins and ends in our own heart. If we can win it there, we will win it in every area of responsibility.

ANOINTING FOR A NEW SEASON

The prophet took Jehu to a private place and anointed him with oil, not only to be king, but also to cleanse his nation from evil. The anointing to lead and to influence inherently carries within it the responsibility to resist the enemy and disempower him. It's vital that leaders understand that the anointing doesn't come from the approval of the people; it comes from being in that private place with the One who calls us. If Jehu hadn't been willing to leave the other warriors in order to go and hear from God, he would not have received the anointing to carry him through the fight that lay ahead. When he came back to the war room, it was obvious that something about him was different, and people quickly caught the vision, surrendering their own plans to receive him as their new leader.

With no time to lose, the company set off immediately for Jezreel for a showdown with evil. The watchman announced their approach, and riders were sent to question their intentions. Peace is such a debatable issue because it is not merely the absence of friction. Peace in a nation relates to the state of being when the people are right with God,

> God blesses those who work for peace, for they will be called the children of God (Matthew 5:9).

In every place and under every regime, there are those who need only the opportunity to hear from a righteous leader that there can be peace when the reign of wickedness is removed. Many don't realize there is an alternative, but something in their hearts waits for someone to come and tell them. As soon as they understand there is another way, they'll join an army of righteous warriors. Those who rode out to question the soldiers' intentions suddenly found a reason for living in a different way and joined with the warriors who were fighting to establish the new season. As John Maxwell so famously says, *"Leadership, first and foremost, is **influence**."*

Christians can be so afraid of those who question what we do and why, not realizing that often the reason they question is to see if there is a cause they can live and die for. Had Jehu shrunk back in fear from clearly stating his mission, they would not have joined him, and the rest of the story would have been quite different.

You Know Who You Are When
You Understand Whose You Are

Finally the king himself rode out to meet the new generation army, but on realizing Jehu's intentions, he tried desperately to escape. Jehu understood his own role in God's purposes, and it was this certainty that gave him the strength and tenacity to follow through on what he had been anointed to do. The king and his cohorts were killed, and Jehu and his army turned their attention to the source of the evil. It is never enough to deal with the flesh-and-blood causes of problems. If the source isn't dealt with, the same evil will spring up again in other guises and other places.

The real enemy of the land at this time was Jezebel, a domineering and amoral woman whose evil is legendary and whose name has come to represent the spirit of control and immorality. Often people mistakenly refer to this spiritual force as "she" because Jezebel was female, but spiritual forces have no gender. They are merely the embodiment of demonic attributes that have no predilection for men or women. Whoever will submit to their control is used by them to destroy the lives of others, and their own lives as well.

As she realized the army of the Lord was approaching, Jezebel took pains to present the strongest face she could muster. The bottom line of all the devil's schemes is intimidation, and in dressing up to meet the followers of a new way, Jezebel attempted to intimidate them, hoping they would draw back from doing what they were well able to do. Calling Jehu a murderer, she likened him to others whose motives were wrong and whose deeds were evil. It is a common ploy of the enemy to accuse people who are doing right of having wrong motives, because threats are often his only chance of aborting the mission. He will risk everything on the hope that we will be intimidated to the point of giving up and backing down. Yet God has called us to bring freedom to the nations, and only as we stand firm in who He has called us to be will we see the break-through. Going back is not an option. Once we've heard the call of God to cleanse the land, we have to go for it, or we will find every-thing we do from that point on loses its power to effect change.

In the same way as others like Nehemiah made the choice to stay focused and not enter into a debate on the rights and wrongs of the mission, Jehu didn't bother to answer Jezebel's accusa-tions. He was not intimidated by her power dressing or her words because his heart remained focused on the fulfillment of his mission. Shouting past her into the tower, he called out, "Who is on my side?" Once again, as happened with the riders of Jezreel, some were listening who had been living as captives for years in that evil place. In the eyes of the world, they were in-significant people—eunuchs, surgically castrated slaves unable to produce life. Like drones, overlooked and of little value, they felt they lived merely to look after the property of their masters.

Christians not only receive the life of Christ, but also the man-date to give it to others…a eunuch can't do that. His capacity to give life has been destroyed by someone else. There are many Christians who feel as though the life has been crushed out of them. It appears they've been so badly damaged by others that their life-giving capacity has been damaged beyond repair; but in Christ, that's not true. Jesus Christ has the capacity to restore us to such a degree that we don't just receive life for ourselves, but we are able to give life also. When we learn what it is to not just re-ceive, but also give the life of Christ, we cross the line into abun-dance of life.

After all those years, those eunuchs suddenly realized they were not powerless—far from it. When they heard that battle call—the warrior cry of a new generation—something on the in-side of them rose up, and they realized they had the power to take authority over the deception and abuse they had been living with every day! They looked out the window at their deliverer, and saw the light in his eyes and felt the heat of the fire in his heart in their own hearts. And when he said, "Throw her down," they did exactly that.

Kicking and screaming, she threatened and shrieked...but they weren't listening to her anymore, because now they could smell the fragrance of freedom that pervades the land when a new influence begins to rise. Tossed out of her house, she landed with a heavy thud in the dust of the road where Jehu's horse trampled her to death. The spiritual force of evil that had influenced the entire nation for more than a generation was destroyed in an instant! Later, when they went to bury her, there was very little left—only her skull, her hands, and her feet. The rest of her body had been eaten by dogs according to the prophecy given by Elijah (see 1 Kings 21:23).

Jezebel is the name some give to the spiritual force behind sexual immorality, controlling influences, manipulation, deception, and addictions; and its sole purpose is to destroy people and nations. However, we who choose to walk in the Spirit need to bear one truth in mind, and that is that the controlling spirit over each nation is the Holy Spirit. It is imperative that we understand and in faith take our part in destroying the spiritual forces that want to kill, steal, and destroy the life and beauty of each nation and their peoples. We are not in an evenly matched fight; this battle is not about yin and yang, or the power of "the force." The power of God is far greater and far more effective than any spiritual force from hell. The battle has already been won by the finished work of Jesus Christ on the cross. The issue lies not with the power of God or the power of the enemy, but in the willingness of the Church to understand who we trust and why.

The eunuchs powerfully illustrate what can happen to those who feel oppressed and held captive to evil when God comes on the scene. They were enslaved in the house that sheltered and protected the very source of the malevolence that was destroying the nation. Up until then, even though they could have combined forces and thrown her out of the window at any point, they felt powerless. They had no frame of reference to understand they could work together to defeat the evil that reigned in the nation...until a new kind of influence arose and they heard its cry! Someone was telling them they could do it; they weren't helpless victims of circumstance, but people who had the power to take authority over the victimization that had dogged their lives and deal with it through the power of God. They took hold of their own destiny with courage and strength and threw the source of evil down out of the place they lived!

DEAL WITH THE ENEMY IN YOUR OWN LIFE FIRST

Let me tell you the secret of destroying the work of the evil one in your area of responsibility, whether that is in your job, your church, your community, your family, or your nation. *Destroy it in your own life first*. This secret was told to me by a dear friend, AnnMarie Seymour, who was the prayer pastor in our church. As she labored in prayer over the district where she lived in New South Wales, Australia, and the church she was part of at the time, God revealed to her that the force gripping the district had its roots in control and manipulation. She attempted to deal with it, but failed. As she continued to seek God, He showed her the areas of control and manipulation in her own heart and her own house. She came to understand that if she was to have the power to deal with it in the spiritual realms over the region she lived in, she must first deal with it in her own house.

The same is true of the Church. If it is to destroy the works of the enemy in a region or nation, it must first deal with those same things in itself. Whatever your own point of reference, you must deal with it there before you can deal with it in your area of responsibility, because the enemy is well aware of the things he is able to snare us with. He laughs in the faces of those who attempt to destroy his work while it's still alive and thriving in their own hearts. Throw it down out of your own house and you will be free to deal with it in the church, the community, and the nation. Unless you can deal with the enemy and break his grip over your own life, you will not have the right to bring freedom in the place God has given you responsibility to cleanse. Unless a church breaks the grip of the enemy in its own sphere, it will never have the power or strength to destroy that work in the nation.

Unless you can deal with the enemy and break his grip over your own life, you will not have the right to bring freedom in the place God has given you responsibility to cleanse. Unless a church breaks the grip of the enemy in its own sphere, it will never have the power or strength to destroy that work in the nation.

When Christians lie and cheat and steal, when they give way to lust, sleep with someone they are not married to, when they walk in pride or fear and say someone else is responsible for their sin, they show themselves to be an emasculated people with no power to live for God. Too often Christians live as eunuchs in the Kingdom of God, having life but unable to pass it on. Living their lives as defenseless victims of the destruction that lives within them in their own home, they fail to understand how easily they could be free. Too often the very evil we've hated in the nation has been resident in our own homes and our own lives, and we've not understood that we have the right and power to deal with it through Jesus Christ.

A person without self-control is as defenseless as a city with broken-down walls (Proverbs 25:28).

Unless we make the choice consistently to go alone to a place where we can hear from God and receive His anointing, unless we deliberately choose every day to walk away from the sin that so easily besets us, we will never have the capacity to throw sin out of our own house and our own lives. We can never throw it out of our family, our job, our church, or our nation until we've dealt with it in ourselves; and that dealing must be a daily habit, because the sin we have dealt with knocks regularly at our door to see if we're still trusting Jesus to keep us clean, or if we may be open to an occasional little flirtation with evil.

Notice that Jezebel's entire body was eaten, with the exception of her skull, her hands, and her feet. These three sets of bones have a powerful imagery for us. The skull speaks of the battle for the mind that all of us who are called as God's influencers must face every day. The feet speak of our walk in Christ, and our hands speak of serving Him. Wherever our minds choose to take us, our feet will walk in that direction, and ultimately, our hands will find ourselves doing those things we have allowed ourselves to think about. The crux of the matter is that even when we deal with the sin in our lives, it is imperative we remember that the skeleton of the enemy lies buried, just waiting for our thought life to put flesh back on the bones again.

In every nation, societies are groaning under the weight of sin. The oppression experienced by all cultures and races goes bizarrely hand in hand with the struggle of a minority to bring the freedom of Christ to everyone...and it has always been this way.

While the battle for human souls rages across the heavens and the earth, most of those over whom it is being fought are totally oblivious to any battle but their own, which is just to survive. The traffic jams, the bills, the life-and-death struggles, and the fight to just wake up again tomorrow, all work together to obscure from view the reality of the war being fought between good and evil. A new generation is rising in response to the call of Jesus Christ; and they rise, not from among the most powerful or charismatic, but out from among those of His people who are willing to be changed, to acknowledge their own sin, and throw it down from their lives regardless of how painful that is and how much anguish it causes.

In order to do a new thing, we must be willing to be a new thing, and the world is waiting for those who not only dare to bring the Savior into their spheres of influence but who also show they can live what they say. It's the time of a new generation Christian, one who can put his mouth, his money, and his actions into the purposes of God for a world who is crying out for a Savior.

CHAPTER TWO

What to Do When God Tries to Kill You

You may have to fight a battle more than once to win it.

Margaret Thatcher

Anyone who makes even the smallest choice to influence others to live for God quickly becomes painfully aware that it is very difficult to practice what you preach...all the time. Try as we may to get what appears to be our final "i" dotted and final "t" crossed in the business of doing God's work in God's way, it is glaringly obvious to others, if not to ourselves, that there remains yet more work to be done.

Many times I have sat opposite someone bemoaning the issues of his or her life and found as they relate their story that some of my problems are the same as theirs, or worse still, I become aware that my own actions are similar to those of the person they are complaining about. Though they may have come to me for answers, if I'm honest, I find the issues they assume I've dealt with are often still alive and well and living comfortably in my heart. Times like that make all of us who want to be catalysts for the purposes of God question our right to influence others when we are still at war with the same issues.

Moses knew this up close and personal. He spent the first 40 years of his life coming to terms with his call as a deliverer of his people, the next 40 years wondering how he could ever have entertained such a ludicrous thought, and his last 40 years being the deliverer he was called to be.

To the Manor Born (Exodus 3:4–4:17)

When God called him, Moses initially refused to believe the Lord could really use him. You'd have to understand his background to see why he felt so strongly about it because it hadn't always been that way. Growing up in a unique and privileged position as Pharaoh's adopted grandson, in his early years he'd been pretty confident. Deep in his heart he was aware that he'd been born for a purpose, and the passing years began to awaken in him an understanding that this involved helping his own race. Though he was a Jew, he was not enslaved like them but was free to go where he wanted and do what he liked. Far from being downtrodden and broken like the rest of his race, he was a member of a royal family—loved, accepted, and powerful in his own right.

As the years went on, he'd become increasingly aware of his own people and understood his true identity as a Hebrew, though it was rarely referred to. One day, aged about 40, curiosity prevailed, and he went to check out the state of the Hebrew nation. He saw their pain and their bondage, and his heart was touched by their plight. Despite his different dress and lifestyle, he felt strangely at one with them. When he saw an Egyptian beating a slave, Moses took the only action he understood—he killed the guy and buried him. Life was cheap in that setting and the arrogance of his position caused him to think this was an acceptable way to deal with the problem.

Being a deliverer is addictive—you can't keep away from the thing you are called to.

Being a deliverer is addictive—you can't keep away from the thing you are called to. The next day he went out again, but this time he found two Hebrews fighting with each other. His growing realization of the value of belonging caused him to wrongly assume that his people would know he wanted to help; they would know his heart and understand he was the deliverer they've been praying for. And so he intervened boldly. But instead of being grateful, they turned on him.

"Who do you think you are?" the man replied. "Who appointed you to be our prince and judge? Do you plan to kill me as you killed that Egyptian yesterday?" (Exodus 2:14a)

If this was a game of Snakes and Ladders, Moses had just landed on the biggest snake on the board and went straight from being the man of power for the hour to being a complete reject! Not only did they not want him as their deliverer, worse, he realized that the word was on the street about what he had done the day before. Then he heard that Pharaoh, his adopted grandfather, had given orders that he be arrested and killed. After all, no matter how much he looked like an Egyptian, when the rubber hit the road, he was now just a Hebrew, not just rejected by them but also hunted as a betrayer of his adopted people.

Escaping Pharaoh's army, he reached Midian where he made friends with Jethro, the local priest, by rescuing his daughters from the local shepherds who were bullying them (being a deliverer is habit-forming), and he settled down there with one of the daughters, Zipporah. Desperately disappointed, frustrated, and feeling like a failure, he was just glad to be in a place where he was accepted. No longer known as a prince or the son of a princess or as a deliverer, for the first time in his life he was finally just himself. Over the next 40 or so years, he gradually let go of all the great ideas he had entertained and accepted the fact that he was better off as he was. He came to terms with the fact that all his youthful ideas and ideals of being a knight in shining armor to a whole nation were just young dreams that bore no resemblance to reality and the day-to-day issues of life, until one day...

THE CALL OF DESTINY

Moses was doing what he did every day—looking after his father-in-law's sheep out in the depths of the wilderness near the mountain of God. Suddenly, the angel of the Lord appeared to him in the flame of a bush, and God got his attention! Calling him over, God proceeded to tell him that He had heard the cries of the Hebrew slaves in Egypt and had come to rescue them and lead them out of Egypt and into the Promised Land. Then He dropped the bombshell....

"Now go, for I am sending you to Pharaoh. You will lead My people, the Israelites, out of Egypt" (Exodus 3:10).

"Whoa...wait a minute," Moses said. "I've been there, done that...Lord. That T-shirt is worn out, just like me. There is no way I can go to Pharaoh. How can You expect me to lead the Israelites out of Egypt? Remember what happened last time I tried all that. Forget it, God!" (see Exod. 3:11).

God answered, "I'm coming with you...and just to prove I'm with you, when you've done it, you will come right back to this place and worship Me" (see Exod. 3:12). The funny thing about God is that His proof mostly happens after the event, when we don't need proof anymore. It's like being vindicated; we long for vindication when we are being misrepresented, but it's not until after it's all over that vindication generally comes, when we don't need it anymore.

Moses argued vehemently, trying to make Him see reason, but in the face of God's persistence, he finally agreed and began on the journey of obedience. Just as he was leaving, the Lord reminded him again of how difficult it would be (see Exod. 4:21). All very encouraging really, just what you need to hear when you had to be talked into going in the first place!

HELP! GOD IS TRYING TO KILL ME

Heading off with his wife and sons, Moses was bound for Egypt, carrying the staff of God; and on the way a very strange thing happened, considering the conversations God had had with him.

> *On the journey, when Moses and his family had stopped for the night, the Lord confronted Moses and was about to kill him. But Zipporah, his wife, took a flint knife and circumcised her son. She threw the foreskin at Moses' feet and said,* **"What a blood-smeared bridegroom you are to me!"** [When she called Moses a "blood-smeared bridegroom," she was referring to the circumcision.] *After that, the Lord left him alone* (Exodus 4:24-26, emphasis added).

On the face of it, these verses don't make sense. God was the One who got Moses' attention at the burning bush; God was the One who talked him into going and who had transformed his shepherd's rod, enabling him to do supernatural things so people would believe he was called to lead; and now God was trying to kill him...and for what? Because his son wasn't circumcised? It seems totally unreasonable...until you look closer.

Part of the Jewish law is that little Hebrew boys are circumcised on the eighth day after their birth; it happens to every son on that day, without exception. Moses would have been circumcised, and everyone knew this ceremony was for a purpose. The trouble is that "purpose" and "religious ritual" often get mixed up. There are many things we do as Christians because it's part of the deal— it's what all Christians do; yet sometimes we have long ago lost the reason for why we do what we do. We just know we should do it.

As a young mother living in a country town in New South Wales, Australia, I was surrounded by a closely connected group of neighbors who were all good friends. One Easter, while talking to my neighbor Alison, it became clear that she felt the Christian thing was to eat only fish on Good Friday. I had not long been a Christian and didn't yet know all the "rules" of the church. I was curious that my church hadn't told me there was a prescribed meal for Good Friday. Alison (who incidentally wasn't a practicing Christian) told me that she knew it was the Christian thing to do because her mother had told her; it was part of their family tradition. I searched my Bible in vain for something to substantiate this strange rule. It's remarkably easy for the church to establish rules that God never gave.

In the same way, we can observe certain Christian sacraments, like communion, in a habitual way while at the same time working out where we will go for dinner, or wishing we'd finished the work the boss had assigned to us before the weekend. We are doing the right thing, but have lost context on why we do what we do. We could explain it easily if someone asked us, yet our hearts are disengaged. Eventually we, or our children who follow us, lose sight of the need to do something that no longer means anything to us.

That may have been how it was for Moses. He was circumcised himself, but he hadn't gotten around to getting his son done. Why not? Maybe Zipporah didn't want him to. She was not a Jew, and it's possible that the circumcision of her first son (they had two boys) may have been so traumatic that she was determined not to allow it to happen to her second baby. Walking the floor with a screaming baby is bad enough when you culturally understand the reason why, but if she felt circumcision was merely a ritual of her husband's religion that had no meaning to her, it seems reasonable that she was determined that the same thing wouldn't happen to the next baby. Moses had never lived as a Jew and may have postponed or decided against circumcising the second baby because he thought it was like eating fish on Good Friday—a traditional ritual but no big deal. Although he was circumcised, he hadn't been brought up in the Hebrew culture and consequently would have missed out on gaining the basic intrinsic understanding of why his people did what they did.

However, it was a big deal, because circumcision represents the Jewish people's acceptance of the covenant with God. The man who was on his way to being God's deliverer of a circumcised people had neglected to value the covenant God had made with them by failing to circumcise his own son and thus negated the very agreement that set them apart from all other nations. In biblical terms, the flesh relates to sin. The cutting away of the flesh on the little Jewish sons of every generation beginning with Abraham represents a deliberate choice by the people of God to remain pure and dedicated to their God.

This is the covenant that you and your descendants must keep: Each male among you must be circumcised; the flesh of his foreskin must be cut off. This will be a sign that you and they have accepted this covenant (Genesis 17:10-11).

That's the Old Testament, but does circumcision relate to Christians? Throughout the Old and New Testaments, circumcision is always understood to symbolize the choice to deal ruthlessly with personal sin.

So circumcise the foreskin of your [minds and] hearts; be no longer stubborn and hardened (Deuteronomy 10:16 AMP).

And the Lord your God will circumcise your hearts and the hearts of your descendants, to love the Lord your God with all your [mind and] heart and with all your being, that you may live (Deuteronomy 30:6 AMP).

These two Scriptures were written to a people who spent 40 years in the wilderness. During that time, perhaps because of being on the move, they had lost the practice of circumcision. Later, when they prepared to take the Promised Land under Joshua's leadership, this was the first thing they had to attend to before they could go in; it was a deliberate realignment with God's promise for the new season.

At that time the Lord said to Joshua, "Make knives of flint and circumcise the [new generation of] Israelites as before" (Joshua 5:2 AMP).

It's obvious that circumcision for adults is a whole lot more painful and incapacitating than it is for babies, but it was vital for these people to acknowledge again their acceptance of the covenant before they went any further in their mission for God. The new generation recalibrated themselves to God's ways through the action of circumcision. They literally reaffirmed their acceptance of the covenant before they began their fight for the Promised Land. Without this obedience of an outward, physical sign that they were set apart from all other peoples, they would not have had God's support to conquer the land and would have failed at the outset of their mission.

Circumcise yourselves to the Lord and take away the fore-skins of your hearts, you men of Judah and inhabitants of Jerusalem, lest My wrath go forth like fire [consuming all that gets in its way] and burn so that no one can quench it because of the evil of your doings (Jeremiah 4:4 AMP).

For Christians, it's a heart attitude rather than physical surgery. So much of what is in our hearts is often left to lie uncircumcised rather than be dealt with and cut out, yet if we don't deal with it ourselves, it will be dealt with by the God who comes as a consuming fire. He gives us the opportunity to deal with our sin before He has to.

> *The issue is that before we can bring deliverance to others, we must be delivered ourselves.*

When you came to Christ, you were "circumcised," but not by a physical procedure. It was a spiritual procedure—the cutting away of your sinful nature (Colossians 2:11).

A true Jew is one whose heart is right with God. And true circumcision is not a cutting of the body but a change of heart produced by God's Spirit. Whoever has that kind of change seeks praise from God, not from people (Romans 2:29).

The issue here is the call of God on the life of anyone who wants to serve Him. Sometimes it takes God a while to talk us into accepting the role He has planned for us since the beginning of time. Moses spent 40 years preparing to be a deliverer, 40 years understanding he never could be, and then 40 years being what God had always destined for him to be. The issue is that before we can bring deliverance to others, we must be delivered ourselves.

We begin by seeing a need, followed by the gradual realization that God is envisioning and equipping us to meet that need. Then we have a go at doing it and fall flat on our face. When we do that enough times, we eventually arrive at the knowledge that we don't have the capacity to do the job, and when we really understand that, God then calls us and commissions us to go and do it.

ON THE ROAD AGAIN

Deliverance is a funny thing. The popular understanding of the word is that you get someone to pray over you, and if you shake, rattle, and roll enough, you'll be delivered. I've seen a lot of that in the years since I've been a Christian, and have often been amazed that in many cases, no matter how many times a person gets delivered from fear, rejection, lust, anger, or whatever else may be his or her problem, those things have a funny habit of returning just as strongly as ever.

It's great to get prayer from other people for these issues; I've done it myself and appreciate that it can often help a great deal with the issues I'm struggling with. However, when it comes right down to it, freedom comes only through one-on-one wrestling with God over the sin, pride, and fear in our hearts, denying ourselves the luxury of maintaining wrong heart attitudes that are destructive. It's in this way that we circumcise our hearts to get rid of the flesh that wants to rise up and cause us to compromise with the sin that's always there, waiting for the weak moments which we inevitably have. Fear is addictive, as are lust and bitterness and anger and whatever else your problem may be. A one-off prayer, no matter how long it lasts or how loud it gets, does not generally mean you never have to deal with your sin again.

When God calls us to serve Him in ways that will bring deliverance and freedom to other people, as soon as He gets our attention and our agreement, He begins to confront us over the areas of sin and compromise in our lives. If you don't know that yet, you aren't doing anything for Him yet. There are points of confrontation that expose the things we are doing that we shouldn't be doing; the things we are not doing that we should be doing; the little hidden things we are playing with; and the places where we are compromising our beliefs in order to be acceptable, comfortable, and in control of our own lives. This confrontation can sometimes make us feel as though we are going to die from the pain we are in.

The problem is that you can't get your heart right in some areas until you're faced with the reasons for it to be wrong.

The thing that was going to kill Moses was that he was about to do God's work without understanding how important his heart attitudes were to the accomplishment of the task. For us, the circumcision of Moses' son relates directly to our need to acknowledge and repent of our wrong attitudes and actions and continue to cleanse our hearts as we journey on to serve Him. The problem is that you can't get your heart right in some areas until you're faced with the reasons for it to be wrong. You can't deal with attitudes you don't know you have. When you make up your mind to serve God and begin to journey down that road, attitudes of pride, fear, unbelief, rejection, anger, bitterness, self-sufficiency, rebellion, and arrogance all rise up in the most incredible ways. We have no way of knowing those attitudes are there until God gets our attention and persuades us to do something for Him.

The feeling that God is trying to kill us doesn't just happen once; it happens over and over again as our profile is raised among our peers and He works with us to expose the areas that need purifying. When He is able to get our attention and agreement, then He begins to expose our own hearts to us. He never really wanted to kill Moses, the guy who was born to be a deliverer of his people, but Moses had to understand the issues of his heart and that it is imperative that God's work is done in God's way.

It's no different for us. Being in a position of authority and responsibility brings out issues in our hearts that would not otherwise arise. That's why God meets us *on the way* as He did with Moses. Many of these issues are not relevant to us until we get on the road to doing what He's called us to. So many people of catalytic influence in the Body of Christ end up faltering and falling through immorality, pride, love of money, or just plain weariness and burnout; and this occurs so often because when God meets them on the way, as He did with Moses, they find ways to avoid dealing with the issues of their hearts.

They continue on the journey, attempting to do the work God has assigned them to in their own way. For a while it may even seem as though they have succeeded, but any unclean vessel that carries the anointing of God will be destroyed by that anointing. Cleanness comes, not through our own perfection, but with deliberate and ongoing choices to deal with the sin that lurks in our hearts when God pinpoints it…on the way. It's all too common to see people the Lord is using brought down by the enemy just because they have made the choice to continue to carry the anointing without continuing to clean up their act by circumcising their hearts.

The Bible says that many are called but few are chosen. How are the choices made as to who will serve God, in what positions, and how effective they will be? Our thinking tends to say that the most gifted and the most capable get the top positions, but in the long term, it's got nothing to do with gifting. God gifts people all over the world, but most people waste their giftings on themselves. The differentiation between the role of "called" giving way to "chosen" is made in the place where you meet alone with God in dead earnest. It's here that you wrestle over your own heart attitudes like Jacob did when he had to acknowledge he was a liar and a cheat; like Moses did when he and his family had to realize that his decision to do less than what God wanted would be

58

enough to not only destroy the mission, but the missionary as well. Our only way to the full-blown purposes of God is through the ongoing decisions we make *on the way* to acknowledge the state of our hearts and allow circumcision to cut away all the stuff that would corrupt and destroy the mission. It's only as we openly acknowledge who we are and what we are doing that we can ever be free to serve Him effectively.

> *Finally, I confessed all my sins to you and stopped trying to hide them. I said to myself, "I will confess my rebellion to the Lord." And You forgave me! All my guilt is gone* (Psalm 32:5).

The world is full of Moses's—people who have come to know Jesus, who were circumcised in the beginning of their relationship with Him, and who have walked in a certain amount of success and blessing as they've been hidden among the people. Many have gone a long way down the track in their faith and are now being called by the Lord to bring deliverance to those who don't know and don't understand God's purposes for them. They are called to bring people out of slavery to sin and teach them how to fight for the uniqueness of what God has given them. If these deliverers fail to understand the ongoing need to circumcise their own hearts and lives, they will fail at their task.

If we want to lead others to walk in freedom, *we must walk in freedom also.* The purposes of God are so often destroyed because of influencers who haven't made the ongoing choices to circumcise their hearts. It's a painful choice to make, but it is the only way forward for a catalyst for God.

CHAPTER THREE

The Purpose of Favor

There is a loftier ambition than merely to stand high in the world. It is to stoop down and lift mankind a little higher.

Henry van Dyke (1852-1933)

One of the major requirements for serving God effectively is His favor. With it, the mission flows; without it, everything is so much more difficult. It is the favor of God that aligns His provision with His purposes. When a person who desires to be a catalyst for God has His favor on their lives, the resources they need will be drawn to them supernaturally. It's an awesome and humbling thing to see the favor of God at work in someone's life and mission, and all the more so when it is painfully obvious that their own ability and resources are incapable of providing what they need to get the job done. It is the favor of God that causes great missions to succeed even though they are mounted by the most ordinary people.

The problem is that people often confuse the favor of God with personality and charisma. It's true that some people naturally seem gifted and blessed, whether they realize that God is at work with them or not. Unfortunately, when favor appears to come naturally, it often removes the person carrying it from the realities of life. Human nature is such that their seemingly charmed existence allows them to think that everyone has it as easy as they do, or worse, that they deserve to have such favor because of some intrinsic superiority of their own. Joseph was one such person, and the Book of Genesis tells the story.

The Amazing Technicolor Dream Coat (Genesis 37:3-4)

Jacob had been cheated by his Uncle Laban. For seven years he had worked hard with the expectation of being given the beautiful Rachel to be his wife. Instead, he was given Leah, the older and far less appealing sister. Ultimately, Jacob ended up with four wives who gave him many sons, but Rachel was always his favorite. As a consequence, her boy Joseph was the son Jacob doted on, and as a mark of his favor, Jacob gave Joseph a wonderful coat, which he wore every day. Wherever he went, everyone could see the outward evidence of his father's love and favor.

It is the favor of God that aligns His provision with His purposes.

Can people see the Father's love on you and me? Do we wear the kind of beauty and grace that doesn't come from our own excellence but from His acceptance of us? Can others strip it from us and force us into a pit? Is it possible that the Father's favor can be snatched away from a person, leaving him or her in prison, enslaved, a victim of chance and circumstance?

Joseph's problem was not so much that he was the favored son; it was that he took full advantage of his position to reinforce his superiority over his brothers. They longed for a coat like that, not so much because of how it looked, but for what it symbolized. They wanted the coat because of the reason Joseph had it—it was a symbol of love, and not just any love, but the love of their father. A father's love is precious because of its crucial role in the shaping of a person's identity. While a mother's love gives us our sense of being, of who we are; to a great degree it is our father's love that gives us our sense of belonging. Without that we continually battle an internal sense of rejection that defrauds us of our sense of identity. We end up in a constant struggle for acceptance rather than being able to rest and enjoy our place in our family and, therefore, in society.

Is it possible that the Father's favor can be snatched away from a person, leaving him or her in prison, enslaved, a victim of chance and circumstance?

Not everyone receives the sort of "belonging love" that only a father can give; Joseph's brothers didn't! They were treated like hired hands instead of heirs, while Joseph was favored; and the world could see that favor wherever he went. It was especially painful for Reuben. As the eldest brother, he was the rightful recipient of his father's favoritism. It was he who should have been given double honor; the coat should have been his, yet it was all given to Joseph because his father loved Joseph's mother more than he loved his other wives.

When a person hasn't been loved in the right way by their dad, he or she often finds it very difficult to relate with the confidence of those who know they are loved. People like that can be really irritating, mainly because of the confidence they walk in. It is clear that they love themselves, and that can be a deep problem to someone who doesn't have the same assurance. To complicate matters, Joseph didn't have the compassion or the maturity to behave in a way that helped his brothers to feel any better about themselves or their role in the family, and so a terrible thing happened. His robe was stolen from him and ruined by the blood that was smeared all over it. Joseph was then pushed into a deep pit and soon sold into slavery where he would learn that the Father's love can't be torn away from us like a garment.

If we will let our circumstances work in us, that sense of love and favor that comes only from God can carry us through whatever happens to us. It can bring us out of the pit and release us from slavery and bondage to sin, as well as all the traps that life sets for us. Even when our circumstances are like a prison, that deep, abiding sense of favor can cause us to live as though we are free. The more Joseph was enslaved, the greater personal freedom he lived in; first the pit, then slavery, and finally imprisoned. It seemed to get worse, but in reality he was increasing in his understanding of what it is to live in the favor of God without the outward uniform!

Not all of us have had the knowledge that our father has loved us unconditionally; not all of us have been able to wear that loving acceptance like a garment for other people to admire and envy. In fact, even for those of us who have, some wrong messages have come through, just as they did with Joseph. At first, instead of assurance, Joseph walked in arrogance and pride. His self-confidence caused him to be insensitive and callous, totally unaware and unconcerned of what life was like for his brothers. He wore his father's love as a badge of superiority instead of having compassion on those who didn't have what he had. He didn't care how life was for them; he thought that all he had and all he was, was for him and because of him. It took the pit, slavery, and the jail for him to finally understand the way a father's love should be worn. It's not to be displayed for our own glory but used to draw other people to the Father.

It is important to walk in the awareness of being loved by God, because somehow that gives us the capacity to love ourselves in a way that we otherwise wouldn't, which is vital; otherwise, if you don't love yourself, God help your neighbor! (see Luke 10:27). The overarching understanding we need is that the Father's love and favor on our lives is not for us but for others—for our family and their families, for our friends and our un-friends, for feeding those we care about and the multitudes we don't even know.

It's true that most of us have not received the fullness of the knowledge of our earthly father's love; and those who have experienced favor have generally interpreted it wrongly, because people who know they are loved often don't have any concept of the pain of un-love. Wearing their garment of love, they take favor for granted, as a right (which it is), without understanding that if it is to stay healthy and clean and do the job it was meant to do, it must be shared with others.

The Kingdom of God has a different culture than the kingdoms of the world. The first gift we receive on our arrival in God's Kingdom is the garment of His love and favor (see Isa. 61:10), but many of us never even try it on. We leave it on the hanger in the back of our faith life. We talk about it and admire it at times, but we don't wear it. There are occasions when we might hold it up against ourselves and look in the mirror. We may even try it on (does my ego look big in this?). But for the most part, we are content to own it but never wear it. The assurance of His unconditional love is such a foreign concept that we're not comfortable wearing it around for others to see, although theologically we can boast that, like a coat in a wardrobe, it is available to us all the time.

He who worked on the massive task of hanging the planets in space and weighing out the seas is, incredibly, captivated by our tiny hearts.

Often, because we've chosen not to wear our own, we tear at the coats of others, pushing them into the same pit we've been desperately trying to claw our way out of. Their stories of faith and answered prayer are a source of envy and disparagement to us. We despise their faith, seeing it as unfounded arrogance, in the same way David's elder brother did when David questioned why no one had yet dealt with Goliath. And all the while we don't realize that God's love and favor can be worn by anyone who has made the choice to accept His free gift of salvation.

The fact is, whatever happened with our own dads, God's love is given full and free to each of us. Each of us is His favorite. That's difficult to get our heads around; but unless we accept it, we will leave the beautiful garment that symbolizes His love as well as his favor hanging in the wardrobe of our lives, and then become overwhelmed with jealousy, self-pity, and indignation when we see others who wear their coats wherever they go. When Jesus Christ died on the cross, it was to make clear once and for all time that we are passionately loved by the Creator of the universe. The One who worked on the massive task of hanging the planets in space and weighing out the seas is, incredibly, captivated by our tiny hearts. His love is poured out on us; we are His passion. The more we come to understand that, the greater will be our ability to wear the amazing coat of His favor and love.

There are also those who, while being aware of the garment of His love and blessing, may act in a way that is unworthy of the concept of that coat. Often, the Church and Christians flaunt God's love without caring about the world at all, and without making any attempt to bless anyone but ourselves. Literally, like

Joseph, we smugly "tell on" others to our Father—*The world does this and that...but we're not like that! Terrorists are like this; my neighbors act like that...but I'm a Christian, Dad. I'm not like that.* We use our relationship with Him to get our own needs met, as though He cares only about us...but that's not the truth. Our Father in Heaven is not like Jacob; He doesn't favor one child above the others. His love and favor are burning and passionate towards each one of us, and yet we thwart and hinder His purposes when we use that favor up on ourselves.

What might have happened if Joseph had used his privileged position to intercede on behalf of his brothers, instead of looking down on them and feeling superior, as though he somehow deserved to be blessed? What would have been the result if he'd taken a picnic and some cold water to them instead of spying on them so he could report back to his dad about how bad they were in comparison to him? Maybe if he'd cared about his unloved brothers, he would never have had to go through all that pain and rejection himself to know what life felt like for them.

> *His love and favor are burning and passionate towards each one of us, and yet we thwart and hinder His purposes when we use that favor up on ourselves.*

Pain has the capacity to teach us how other people feel, and gives us the opportunity to choose between hardening our hearts even more to care only for ourselves, or allowing our pain to teach us how to care for others. When someone has made the decision to be a catalyst for the purposes of God, she allows God to change her heart in the way He changed Joseph's heart, and many people will find their own freedom and release through that person's willingness to be used. Hearts that are starving for love will be filled as we use our own position of grace and favor to bless, instead of to judge; to give, instead of to take; to encourage, instead of inform on.

DREAMS COME TRUE

Joseph's brothers didn't recognize him, but Joseph recognized them. And he remembered the dreams he had had many years before (Genesis 42:8-9a).

It's amazing what a few years of suffering can do for a person, if we let God use that time to teach us. When he saw his brothers bowing down to him, it all came back to him. Here was the embodiment of the dream he'd had as a child. As they talked among themselves, it was obvious they knew they were in this situation now because of how they'd treated Joseph (see Gen. 42:21). They were panicking as they discussed the mess they were in and clearly saw their current situation as payback for what they'd done to their brother all those years before. But the Joseph who listened to their conversation was different from the man they had thrown in the pit. He had changed much, because now he also knew what it was to suffer. Rushing from the room, he found a place where he could weep over them as they struggled in their fear and desperation (see Gen. 42:24).

Joseph was a strategist, and the story still had some time to serve before all could be known. After Joseph sent his brothers away with the vital food in their sacks, they were shocked to find on their way home that their payment for the grain had been returned to them. When the food ran out, Jacob was faced with the heart wrenching choice of starvation for the whole tribe, or losing the last son of his favorite wife. Reluctantly, he agreed that Benjamin could go to Egypt.

Joseph greeted the brothers with great dignity, wining and dining them, and they were astonished to find themselves seated according to their ages. When they left the following day, their money was again returned, and Joseph's personal silver cup was secretly placed in Benjamin's sack. They were barely out of the city when Joseph's servant reached them with accusations of the theft, and the cup was found in Benjamin's sack.

Judah faced with the prospect of leaving his little brother behind and realizing this would cause their father's death, interceded for Benjamin, begging for mercy. The words he used are very telling for us also.

> *Our father's life is bound up in the boy's life* (Genesis 44:30b).

Are we aware of the degree to which our Father's love is bound up in our lives? The price He paid by sending His only Son to die for us means that from that point on, His life has been inextricably bound up in ours. When a person realizes the full depth of this love and the amazing power it has to reach every part of our hearts, his life is changed forever.

Finally, it was time, and Joseph broke the news to his brothers. Sending his attendants out of the room, he broke down and wept as he told them that he was their brother, but no word of recrimination passed his lips. He didn't harangue them or crow over them. He didn't remind them of the dreams he'd had and rub their noses in the humiliation and fear they now felt as they witnessed the fulfillment of those dreams. Rather, his words formed one of the greatest passages in the Bible and serve as encouragement to everyone who has been justly or unjustly dealt with in the house of our friends and family.

> *But don't be angry with yourselves that you did this to me, for God did it. He sent me here ahead of you to preserve your lives. God has sent me here to keep you and your*

families alive so that you will become a great nation (Genesis 45:5,7).

Initially, Joseph had needed to flaunt a special coat to show that he was loved, favored, and equipped to rule. That coat was now long gone, but it was no longer necessary anyway because Joseph had changed so much—who he was destined to be he had now become. No longer spoiled and arrogant, using up the favor of his father on himself, he was now giving all that he had become to help them. His heart attitude was that although their intentions were evil, God was in charge all the time. He could see the hand of God in all the things he had gone through, understanding they had happened in order that he would be where he was needed when the time came. He was sent ahead of his family so that they would be saved and would reach their destiny to become a great nation. The depth of this revelation was so extreme that without the dealings of God to change his heart over all the years of his servitude, he would never have understood why he'd experienced the things he'd lived through.

No longer spoiled and arrogant, using up the favor of his father on himself, he was now giving all that he had become to help them.

Then Joseph kissed each of his brothers and wept over them, and then they began talking freely with him (Genesis 45:15).

Why could they now talk freely with him? Because Joseph had changed! As is common with all of us, he had entirely misunderstood his dreams when he first dreamed them. He thought that being in an exalted position was a mark of superiority, which gave him power to be spent on himself. It took all those years of pain and suffering to bring him to understand the reasons why God calls ordinary people to be catalysts to bring others to their destiny. Favor is never for ourselves; it's always to be used so that the purposes of God can be fulfilled in the lives of others. We make a mistake when we misunderstand God's hand on our lives. In every case, when the Bible speaks of God raising someone up, it was done for the sake of others. It is our privilege to be used of God, and even the hard and inexplicable things we go through have a purpose if we will allow God to use them.

We all can give reasons why we shouldn't always have to be the one who has to change; but when God raises up a catalyst; it's to send them ahead of those He wants to help. At the time, being sent ahead may look like a pit, traps, bondage, and prison; but if we will allow suffering, isolation, and fear to work maturity of faith in our lives, it will become clear that the favor of God is never expressed by what we wear or by how blessed we appear to be. God's favor will truly be shown by who we have become, because our favor will have been put to work on behalf of those whom we have been sent ahead of! Our favor will show the marks of our own efforts on behalf of others.

Your district, your nation, your place of work is teeming with people that you have been sent ahead of. You have the Father's love; you can wear it as a garment any time and all the time if you choose to. But like Joseph, each of us must make the choice whether to just be an informer on those whom God has sent us ahead of, or whether we will become the face of God to them. It's our own choice. So often our irritation with people at work or in our neighborhood or our family causes us to spend our time complaining to God about them and about our circumstances, when all the while He is trying to use our lives and the favor that is intrinsically ours, to be the answer to those people's lives.

You have had your share of difficulties...everyone has. You may have suffered the pain of a family breakup, a dysfunctional background, of sickness, or abuse, or financial trauma. Whatever your personal pit or prison, if Jesus Christ has set you free of it, you have the capacity to help others because you know what it is to go ahead of them.

The reason we're blessed is to be a blessing (see Gen. 12:2), not so the favor we enjoy can be swallowed up on ourselves and those who are dear to us. Most churches have awesome visions to reach their community and beyond, but the success of that vision requires each individual Christian to make his or her own decision to be a catalyst for God to the world, not flaunting our favor, but sharing it with everyone we come across. The world doesn't need any more mean-spirited, arrogant, complacent Christians who think their favor is for themselves and who are praying to see everyone else get their comeuppance. It needs people who know God's love and who are willing to wear the favor and share the favor with people who don't have it.

In the end, Joseph understood that, and he not only saved his brothers and their families from starving to death, he also preserved the destiny that God had promised to them. Without the situations Joseph lived through, the Israelites would never have been saved in the time of famine. It's hard to understand at times why we have gone through some of the things that have happened to us, but God is the ultimate Recycler. If we allow Him to, He has the power to take what has been destruction to us, and convert it into something that can make us grow strong and healthy in His purposes.

CHAPTER FOUR

What You're Feeding Is Breeding

What we make room for, lives with us.

Anonymous

Not one of us came into the world by accident, not even if our parents didn't plan us, or we were the wrong gender, or even if our birth was embarrassing or inconvenient to them. God knew us before the time we were conceived, and He set us apart right then with a plan for how we could serve Him and His people. The trouble is we so often feel that we are not good enough, that we don't fit with the people around us as we are, and that God wouldn't want to use us, so we embark on a total image makeover in order to become acceptable to everyone else.

We alter major aspects of our lives, chopping off pieces of our personality in one area and adding rehearsed characteristics

We have become the image that has been formed over the process of time by our attempts to fit in and be accepted; we are shaped by the values of our environment, and many of those values are false. What we are not is the person God intended us to be when He created us.

somewhere else. We suck in one part of ourselves as though it was a pot belly, and augment other areas with something like silicon implants in order to gain acceptance from people. We're afraid people will reject us if we are just ourselves…if we even knew what that was.

Proverbs 29:5 (paraphrased) says, *"The fear of man is a trap,"* and it's true that we are often trapped by our fear of rejection into being someone we're not, and then we get frustrated with the results. We say "yes" when we mean "no," and then we complain about being too busy. We say "no" when we want to say "yes," and then we are hurt because people don't understand what we want. Friendships are ruined by misunderstanding because we judge ourselves by our intentions and everyone else by their actions. We feel fragmented and alienated, struggling constantly to communicate with God and people, and all because we are not comfortable in the uniqueness of who we were created to be. We have become the image that has been formed over the process of time by our attempts to fit in and be accepted; we are shaped by the values of our environment and many of those values are false. What we are not is the person God intended us to be when He created us.

"For I know the plans I have for you," says the Lord. "They are plans for good and not for disaster, to give you a future and a hope" (Jeremiah 29:11).

He has a specific plan for our lives, but that plan hinges on our relationship with Him. We all have the capacity to be what God has called us to be, but many of us never arrive at that place because of jealousy, envy, bitterness, fear, anger, inadequacy, ambition, pride, lust, and self-pity. And even though we struggle to do the right thing, modifying our behavior and trying to do better next time, we keep finding ourselves falling back into that black hole of failure. The definition of insanity is to keep doing the same thing while hoping things will turn out differently. We can never rescue ourselves, though for some reason we keep hoping we can.

Relationship with Jesus Christ is intended to give abundant life, but lots of Christians go their whole lives without ever experiencing that. Why? It's not to do with things around us, our circumstances, our finances, our partners, our jobs, our talents or gifts. Abundance resides in our inner life; it is the hidden treasure of our hearts. God does not call us to be like the person we most admire, though we often try desperately to be that. The reason all our efforts are in vain is because He wants us to be like Him, not someone He created.

Underground Danger

Several years ago and probably still now enjoying reruns on cable channels, there was a TV series called "Sliders." The premise of the story was based around a group of time and space travelers journeying to different worlds by means of fractures between worlds. One episode so clearly encapsulates my point that, despite its profound implausibility, I simply have to use it.

The sliders had arrived in a new place, a small country town much like any other, except for the fact that all of its citizens were young. The source of this eternal youth turned out to be a gel-like substance extruded by a worm that had mutated after an atomic explosion. The local people ate this gel every night, and it gave them eternal youth. The unfortunate side effect was that the monster's diet was human beings. However, the local sheriff found an answer to the worm's need for people and his own need to keep nosy troublemakers from cashing in on their secret. Strangers quickly became worm food. Moreover, the arrival of the sliders was timely, because of late the monster had been more hungry than usual, and they'd lost a few of the townsfolk.

One of the sliders was caught by the monster and taken to its underground cave. Fortunately, the rest of the group managed to find him, along with several other people, wrapped in cocoons lining the walls of the lair. There was a fight between the bad guys and the good guys, but the good guys eventually escaped, blowing up the cave in the process, together with the monster who was busily engaged in eating the sheriff. The linchpin of the story was that the worm was a female, and the reason more people had been taken lately was because she had just laid a whole load of eggs and was storing up food for her babies when they hatched. The sheriff, who was fighting so hard to preserve the monster and the amazing lifestyle she gave to their town, had no idea that under the surface of his perfect world were developing enough monsters to not only consume the whole town, but the entire planet.

What are you feeding in the subterranean areas of your life? Are you feeding love, forgiveness, encouragement, righteousness, mercy, diligence, courage? Or are you feeding pride, bitterness, dishonesty, resentment, arrogance, double-mindedness, self-pity, anger, lust, ego? If you're human, it's likely to be a bit of both, but make no mistake—whatever you are feeding right now is breeding. It's not enough to merely look good on the surface of your life, because things that are hidden will ultimately always show themselves. To be right on the outside, it is imperative that we sort out the inside, and that's an undertaking that involves regular, consistent, and honest dialogue with God.

David had regular opportunities to learn this lesson. He was a man of great courage and faith in God, but he also got it wrong at times, as we all do, and had to learn what it was to hear from God rather than just go ahead and do God's work in his own way. One such time was when he made up his mind that the presence of God should be resident in his city during his reign as king. This was a great and godly ambition, but unfortunately, he didn't stop to find out from God how he should do that. Often we learn how to do the right thing by doing it wrong first.

Often we learn how to do the right thing by doing it wrong first.

CARRYING GOD'S PRESENCE (I CHRONICLES 13:2-3,7-14)

The ark of the covenant, which housed the presence of God, had been placed outside of Israel for over 20 years. It had been captured by the Philistines when Eli and his sons were priests in the temple and Samuel was a young boy. Both of Eli's sons had died in the battle and Eli himself, on hearing the news that the ark had been captured, fell off his seat and broke his neck because he was not only very old, but also very fat. On the same day, his daughter-in-law died in childbirth, naming her son *Ichabod*, which means, "Where is the glory?" symbolizing that Israel's glory had gone from them when the ark was stolen (see 1 Sam. 4–5).

As was the habit of conquering armies, the Philistines had placed the ark in the temple of their own god, Dagon, but the presence of the true God had caused the statue of Dagon to fall facedown in its own temple twice; the second time it was left beheaded in front of the ark. After that, plague struck all the Philistine towns in the region, and no matter where the ark was sent, the plague continued to break out. In panic, the Philistines made a brand-new cart to carry the ark away from them. It arrived at Kiriath-Jearim where it stayed 20 years.

Because David had a deep desire and love for God, he was determined to bring the ark of God's covenant with His people back into their nation and that his reign be symbolized by the presence of God. He understood that religion isn't enough; nothing genuinely blesses or satisfies the human heart in the way that the presence of God can. Subsequently, in consultation with the priests and population, they concluded that a new cart would be the best method for the job. They had no idea of the degree to which they were being affected by peer pressure. The ark had never been carried like that until the Philistines, who had no idea of the ways of God, had done it that way; yet Israel chose the Philistine method above the instructions that God had given to them.

We often have no idea the degree to which people we have nothing in common with are influencing our decisions and dictating how we do what we do. The idol that Aaron made when the Israelites demanded to see the God that had brought them out of Egypt was a golden calf. Egypt was full of golden calves that people worshiped. Did he realize he was subconsciously copying the god of the Egyptians when he attempted to placate the Hebrews? People everywhere have an innate need to worship something, but what we worship is powerfully influenced by our environment unless we have taken the time to fix the reality of God and His ways into our hearts. A catalyst is a tiny force for change which, when introduced to a circumstance, can totally transform the situation without itself being changed. For this to happen, we have to be convinced of what we believe to such a degree that it is not negotiable. As catalysts for the purposes of God, it is vital that we interact with our world rather than avoid it; yet when Christians have sex outside of marriage, or cheat on their taxes, or lie and gossip and chase after money, we are being influenced rather than being an influence.

The new cart that David had made was timber; what is your cart made of? Maybe it's been some time since you really felt God with you, but you long to be close to Him. What do you do to bring that to pass? Often, we work out what a Christian should do and then do that. We put on our best behavior to impress God and the people around us and hope that we are good enough to make it work.

In one church we attended, a person showed how spiritual they were by speaking quietly, never raising their voice or getting excited about anything; Christians in their view, were created to be a whiter shade of pale. In another church, the new cart that shows you carry the presence of God means being excited all the time about everything, and carrying a funky-looking Bible; you may not read it, but it looks good. It may mean volunteering for every ministry need in the church, or it may mean joining the pastor and all the spiritual people on a 40-day fast. Whatever it is, if it's just an effort to be acceptable to God, it won't work. It will kill your joy, and maybe kill you as well.

In the course of the journey, with God's presence on the brand-new cart, the yoke of oxen stumbled, and Uzzah, with the best intentions, put his hand on the cart to steady it over the potholes. He was instantly struck dead. I've always thought that was a little extreme of God. After all, Uzzah and David were only doing the best they understood.

The problem was that the Israelites had forgotten how to carry God. Peer pressure (also known as tradition) had taken the place of God's instructions. David and his men were energetic and enthusiastic, but energy and enthusiasm quickly become defensiveness and anger when our good works don't work and all our efforts result in failure. Those of us with a reasonable amount of experience in serving God can understand how that feels. There have been times when we have done our best to serve God, but it all went sour and we ended up like David—confused, frustrated, and afraid to try again. *How can I serve the Lord? How can I possibly have His presence in my life? There's no way I can live up to His requirements; I don't even understand what they are.* How often have we been angry with God because our efforts have failed to please Him and we don't understand why? *I was only doing it for Him; I was just trying to please Him. I built Him a new cart, for heaven's sake! What does He want from me?* Most of us have been in David's situation—confused, angry, and afraid, yet still loving God and wanting to serve Him.

The problem is, other people may have their new cart, but God's people may not. Our only option is to do it His way or not at all. He will not permit a new cart to do the job, even though it looks great, nor will He allow our hand to steady His presence. David was doing the right thing the wrong way. It is entirely possible for a person to know they need God with them, but only meet failure when they try to make it happen themselves. When we don't feel His closeness, it's so easy to build a new cart to try and get Him to return. A new cart is anything people do or churches do to try to make God come to us and bless us.

If you look for Me in earnest, you will find Me when you seek Me (Jeremiah 29:13).

We find God through seeking Him, no other way. He doesn't come to us because of our good behavior, or because we are able to cover our sin up in front of Him or other people, or through doing church overtime, or even through praying more, harder, and longer. He only comes as we seek Him.

The ark made a detour and was parked at Obed-Edom's house for three months during which time the Lord blessed the entire household. The story didn't end there, however much Obed-Edom probably wanted it to, because the presence of God is not meant to be kept within the household; it's intended for our entire sphere of influence. Christians who enjoy the blessing of God's presence and keep it safe in their own lives and in their own families miss out significantly on the greater blessing of bringing the presence of God into their community and nation. As the new ruler of Israel, David knew that it was his responsibility to make sure that God's presence was at the heart of the nation and in the seat of government. Because his heart was committed to God, he knew he had to find a way to enable that to happen, but now he also understood that you can't just decide to do something for God and then work it out yourself. Doing His work our way will never succeed. Humility and willingness to learn and change are what is required to stay with what God is doing in any season.

FOR GOD'S SAKE (1 CHRONICLES 15:1-4,11-16,25-29)

David was a teachable person, so when he tried again three months later, he was ready to follow God's instructions. He invited everyone to come so that they all could have the opportunity to take part in what God was doing. This time the priests placed the ark on their shoulders by using poles threaded through rings so they could carry the presence of God without touching it with their own hands.

Shoulders always symbolize government, support, and strength in responsibility. The presence of God can be carried only by those who will take priestly responsibility for it, determining that God will get the glory and not ourselves. The anointing of God will ultimately destroy anyone who tries to do it any other way. That's why we hear of people whose ministry involves amazing gifts of healing and even miracles, and yet behind the scenes their personal life is in tatters. Their character may be deeply flawed by things such as immorality, pride, and mishandling of their God-given authority, and yet they continue to operate great signs and wonders. These people often continue to have a strong following even by those who can see that the base is all wrong, under the mistaken impression that the miracles mean that God is still with them.

> *For God's gifts and His call can never be withdrawn* (Romans 11:29).

Before a person is formed in the womb, God has already planned who they are to be. While all Christians are encouraged to lay hands on the sick to see them recover, there are those who are given gifts of healings (see 1 Cor. 12:9), specifically, as their job description in the Body of Christ. However, the Bible also makes it clear that gifts are given, not earned because of spiritual superiority, and operating in spiritual gifts is not an indicator of spiritual health (see 1 Cor. 12:2; Matt. 7:21-23). Our gifts are given to us freely and undeservedly. Having them and operating them doesn't mean we are more spiritual or stronger Christians; they are simply gifts that are given to us for the purpose of building up the Body of Christ. Paul puts it beautifully when he says, "What makes you better than anyone else? What do you have that God hasn't given you?" (1 Cor. 4:7a). The only thing we can do in relation to our gifts is to take responsibility to hone and develop them, to bring them from immaturity to increasing maturity; but we can't manufacture or earn them.

On the other hand, the development of our character is our responsibility. Gifts are given, but fruit grows; and the fruit of the Spirit must be prolific in our lives so that we will operate the gifts and authority effectively with right motives rather than serve our own, often unconscious ends. That doesn't mean that we have to be perfect to exercise them; we'd be waiting a long time if we were waiting for that, but it does mean that our heart's intentions must be consistently brought before the Lord for correction and adjustment.

God helped the priests carry His presence (see 1 Chron. 15:15,26-28). As they walked that long journey, carrying their precious but exceedingly heavy cargo, inlaid with gold as it was, God kept them from stumbling because they were obeying His instructions. They danced all the way, laughing, singing, and shouting praise to the Lord. David danced more than anyone else that day. Although he was a warrior, he was not wearing his armor; although he was a king, he was not wearing his king's robes. He understood that no matter what our earthly roles are, we are all equal in the eyes of God. No one of us is preferred above the others regardless of our ministry gifting or calling; we all are worshipers of a King and God who alone deserves the glory.

INTIMATE BUT BARREN

David's wife, Michal, who was watching through a window upstairs (see 1 Chron. 15:29), was much like many Christians. A king's daughter, she had been bought with blood (in her case, the price was the foreskins of 200 Philistines; in ours, the blood of Jesus Christ), and she was now married to the king. What was she doing up there looking out a window when she should have been down with everyone else celebrating the return of the presence of God to their nation? She didn't see the reason for their joy; all she saw was a bunch of idiots dancing and making themselves look ridiculous. This was especially true of her husband, whom she despised. She totally missed the significance of what God was doing. Why?

Michal's life had not been easy, as most of ours have not been either. She'd been deeply in love with David, and had laid her life on the line to help him escape from her father. After he had left, she'd been devastated; but then her father had given her to another man, and somehow she'd been able to put the pieces of her life back together. Her husband, Paltiel, though neither a king nor a great warrior as David had been, was nevertheless good and kind. He loved her, and slowly her broken heart was healed; and she began to enjoy her life, her marriage, and her circumstances.

All that had ended when David came back triumphantly into the city. In the process of reclaiming the throne, he also reclaimed the wife he'd left behind. However, now things were different. No longer the young minstrel who had charmed her heart with his music, he was now a hardened warrior. Even worse, her place as his only wife had been usurped by not one but several other women for whom it was clear he had deep affection. She had not only lost Paltiel, a dear and loving husband who had run weeping down the road after her when she was taken from him; she'd also lost her role as David's only love. If anyone had reason to be resentful, it would seem to have been Michal.

However, every one of us has reason to be resentful. The circumstances of living are such that everyone can recount stories of hurt and suffering that have given them great reason to be bitter. It is said that it is not what happens to us that dictates who we are and what our future will be, but what we do with what happens to us.

Michal's situation was painful, as all of us can relate to at various levels; but she'd been feeding disappointment, rejection, bitterness, and fear for so long she couldn't get out of the habit of it, and what she was feeding had been breeding. Because of her perspective on the wrong side of the window, she was totally unaware of the presence of God or of her need of His presence. Because of this, she suffered a terrible fate. Though she remained the king's wife forever, because of her focus on herself rather than God's plan for her life, she was barren to the day of her death.

How tragic to live in a relationship that should be the most intimate love we could know, and not bear fruit from it. Wholeness is one of the most valuable personal assets we can possess, but wholeness comes through intimacy. Only as we relate fully and openly with Jesus who bought us with His own blood can we find real wholeness. Our hearts will continue to breed discontent and bitterness unless we make the decision to change what we feed ourselves and choose to feed the things that God wants to do in us, despite the pain of our circumstances and the reasons why we shouldn't have to.

What I allow to breed in my heart is a matter of choice. I know the things my emotions want to feed. Feelings will always pull us toward rejection, hurt, envy, anger, or pride; and sometimes the temptation to feed those things is so strong it seems that we don't have the capacity to do anything other than what our feelings dictate. The only way out of this is through doing what David did, which is to seek God, determining to bring His presence into our life and circumstances. That's the only way we can get the strength to choose what we will feed our inner life, and it is vital that we make the choices to do this, because whatever we are feeding…is breeding!

CHAPTER FIVE

Being a Victim Ain't All It's Cracked Up to Be

Faith is a living, daring confidence in God's grace, so sure and certain that a man could stake his life on it a thousand times.

Martin Luther

Anyone who has been a Christian for even a short period of time will have observed a strange phenomenon in the Body of Christ. I have known many people whose hearts truly long to see God glorified and whose lives are given to serving Him—people who really want to do things His way, who desire above everything else to see His Kingdom established through their lives, and who understand that the grace of God alone can enable them to do it...and yet they have felt they have failed miserably. I've watched people struggle to reach new places in God, to live their lives for His glory, only to end up feeling inadequate and unfit for service. Disillusionment and death of hope so easily grips the lives of good, godly people who totally believe in the grace and unmerited favor of God, and I have seen their despair as they have made the decision to give up trying because it has become clear to them that they do not have what it takes to make it in their own eyes, in other people's eyes, and, they think, in God's eyes. I have never failed to grieve deeply over what I've seen, and all the more because I see the same tendencies in myself to let go and give up despite my awareness that only God can do it in me, and only as I keep leaning into Him can I succeed at serving Him. There is nothing as heartbreaking as the loss of good men and women who have responded to the call of God but then concluded that they don't have what it takes to do what they've been called to do and have lost understanding that the grace of God means He is on our side to help us.

A Victim Mentality

There is one common denominator among all these broken people, and it attacks the life and efforts of every Christian with the specific intention of demoralizing and destroying the life of Christ at work in them. That single factor is hurt.

Hurt surrounds us. We see it everywhere, even in the church. It invades our space; it nullifies so many of our good choices and actions; it twists and turns in our hearts like a knife blade and leaves us feeling broken, bitter, and bereft. Our Christian walk can be rendered lame and ineffective by the effects of hurt on our life, and the worst of it is that we so often have no idea what to do about it. Jesus has a solution for hurt, but it is a solution that requires something from us. He is willing to heal us, but we must have the courage to receive the healing. There is a story of Jonathan's son who was deeply wounded in his childhood in a way that threatened to ruin his life.

Saul's son Jonathan had a son named Mephibosheth, who was crippled as a child. He was five years old when Saul and Jonathan were killed at the battle of Jezreel. When news of the battle reached the capital, the child's nurse grabbed him and fled. But she fell and dropped him as she was running, and he became crippled as a result (2 Samuel 4:4).

Mephibosheth was just a kid, a little boy who didn't belong in a hostile environment. One minute he was playing happily with his nurse; and the next minute he was in her arms, and they were running for his life. Saul and Jonathan had been killed, and civil war had broken out in Israel between the house of Saul and the house of David. No heirs to the throne were safe in that sort of environment, and the nurse was desperate to make sure the little prince's life was saved. Amid the chaos and in her mad panic to get her charge to safety, he was dropped, and his feet were irreparably damaged. From that day on, not only was he lame, but his entire life changed. He'd been a healthy, privileged little boy, the grandson of a king, and possibly heir to the throne; now he was an orphan, limping through life as a fugitive. Despite that fact that he was taken into Machir's home and given love and shelter, he nurtured in his heart the sense that he was a victim of life and circumstances, and in this way a mind-set began to develop in his thinking through which his image of himself was formed.

Jesus has a solution for hurt, but it is a solution that requires something from us. He is willing to heal us, but we must have the courage to receive the healing.

RE-BREAKING THE BROKENNESS

At age 22, I contracted cancer and spent my birthday in the hospital having an operation for melanoma, the result of years before suntan lotion was known to be a summer necessity in Australia. The lady in the next bed was a Polish woman in her late 60's who was having an operation on her feet. When she was a small child, war had broken out in Eastern Europe, and Poland was invaded. All the people in the village turned out to watch as the army trucks and tanks went rumbling through their village. The road was crowded, and she was jostled forward just as a truck drove past and ran over her feet. There were no doctors or medications available to her village at that time and over a period of months, her feet healed in the position they'd been crushed into. Like Mephibosheth, she was lame from that time on.

There are many people like Mephibosheth. None of us have been born into the perfect family, and our surroundings and various circumstances affect us as we grow up, which we carry with us into our adulthood. In a variety of different ways, whether because of a crisis or just day-to-day living, we all have experienced the sensation of being dropped and made lame. It may have been accidental as it was with Mephibosheth, or the result of cruelty or a dysfunctional family, but lameness can be so easily thrust upon the life and vitality of a person who doesn't understand what has happened or why.

As was often the custom in those days, this little boy had two names, and it's interesting to note what they mean. *Mephibosheth* means "greatly ashamed" and "confusion," and this name was embodied in who he became after his accident. He must have felt incredibly troubled over the sudden change of circumstance, and a typical response of anyone to such situations is often shame and confusion.

We are called by God to a divine purpose, but stuff happens; we lose our job, or we lose a relationship, we suffer abuse or our finances fail, and we find ourselves living with a shame that is so deeply entrenched in who we are that we may not even recognize it as shame. Instead, we feel inadequate, or we suffer from rejection with all its attendant companions, such as oversensitivity, defensiveness, self-aggrandizement, recklessness, or the constant need to prove ourselves to other people. Added to that, we struggle with confusion as we endeavor to make sense of our lives, wondering why we have become what we have become.

Mephibosheth's other name was *Meri-Baal*, which means "quarreler" or "to wrangle, to disperse strife." Our enemy wants to tear, divide, and quarrel with God's people, and that enemy is never another person despite how much it often appears that way. The Bible says the devil has come to kill, steal, and destroy (see John 10:10), and he will use any means, any people, even parents and friends, teachers and strangers, to bring about his degrading purposes. It may even be the church which has hurt us so much, or the pastor, or someone we have cared for or mentored. These things are relatively common, but it is vital that we remember that our enemy is never our brother or sister no matter what the provocation. Our enemy is always the evil one who sometimes is able to use people who are close to us to attack us and bring us down.

GRACE AND RESTORATION

Israel was now in civil war, as the house of Saul and the house of David battled against each other for supremacy and the right to rule the nation. You may have been caught in a civil war; your parents' marriage broke up, or maybe your own marriage failed, or your church split and everyone took sides and you felt caught in the middle, or some similar thing. It was probably no one's intention to harm you, but in the chaos you were somehow dropped and lameness has come upon you.

As time went on, a measure of healing came to Mephibosheth. The damaged bones healed so that he could walk, but still he limped badly. Many of us suffer in the same way after we've been dropped—we can walk through life, but with difficulty and pain. Yet it's God's intention to bring total, not partial healing. David is a type of Christ, and we gain insight into the nature of God when we look at the grace with which He dealt with Mephibosheth's situation.

HONORING THE HOUSE OF SAUL (2 SAMUEL 9:3-11)

David was a man with a generous spirit who had a real love for people. He had always loved Saul, even though Saul's jealousy and insecurity had prevented him from understanding that. Now that the battle was over and David was king of Israel, he determined to give honor to Saul's house and he made enquiries about how he could do that. He was thrilled when he was told of Mephibosheth, the son of his dearest friend, and he immediately brought him into his palace, treating him as though he were his own son. He restored to him everything that would have been his had the war never taken place.

It's interesting to notice how Mephibosheth felt in this situation. He'd been entertaining self-pity, confusion, and contention for years, which had allowed a strong mind-set to shape his view of himself. Now, just being in the presence of the king made him feel even more worthless; he felt as though he was the lowest of the low. He should have grown up to be confident, strong, and powerful, but instead, he felt like a dead dog in the presence of the one who just wanted to love him. Rather than embracing the restoration of his position and taking the opportunity to grow in health and confidence, he continued to see himself as lame. Though his lameness was real, it had become his reason for not getting on with his life.

All through the Bible we see that God wants to heal lameness and brokenness. He sees how crippled certain areas of our lives have become, but His desire is to heal and restore. However, it's the choice of the individual to receive that restoration, and the way that person is able to follow and serve Jesus Christ hinges on whether he or she is able to accept the grace He extends with enough courage to allow themselves to be changed and infused with the strength to follow Him.

THE TEST OF DISCIPLESHIP

A while later, the tide of public opinion turned against David, forcing him to leave Jerusalem. His son Absalom had mounted a coup with the intention of assuming the throne (see 2 Sam. 16:1-4). As David left the city, Mephibosheth's servant Ziba, the one who had been steward of all Saul's property until Mephibosheth's reappearance, came out to meet him with some donkeys and some provisions. When David enquired about Mephibosheth's whereabouts, Ziba lied saying that he had stayed behind boasting that God was about to restore the kingdom of Saul to him. David was already deeply wounded by his own son's betrayal, and it wasn't difficult for him to believe that everyone had turned against him, so he told Ziba that he could have Mephibosheth's property back, which was Ziba's plan all along. David had other things on his mind and didn't think through the fact that what Ziba said was totally out of character for Mephibosheth who didn't have the personal strength or courage to stand against Absalom.

Though his lameness was real, it had become his reason for not getting on with his life.

When Absalom was defeated and David came back to reclaim his kingdom, Mephibosheth came out to meet him (see 2 Sam. 19:24-30). It was clear from his appearance that he had been in mourning. He had not washed himself or cut his hair or nails since the day David had left the city. It was also clear that he had no thought of taking David's throne; his victim mind-set meant that he never would have had personal capacity or the manpower to stand up against Absalom even if he had wanted to. When David asked why Mephibosheth had not supported him in his hour of need, he replied that he was too lame to follow David himself but had sent Ziba to represent him and that Ziba had lied. In the end, and probably frustrated at Mephibosheth's self-pitying focus on himself rather than the issues of the kingdom and his loyalty to his king, David commanded that the property be divided among them equally. Ziba may not have been the most honest person in the story, but at least he had the guts to stand with David in his hour of need.

Mephibosheth's issues did not lay in his love or loyalty for David; the problem was in how he saw himself even after grace had been extended to him. His status as a crippled orphan made him feel worthless and unlovable, even while David had acted as a type of Jesus in restoring his property and giving him a place at the king's table, treating him like one of his own sons. In reality, the Kingdom of Heaven had come through David to Mephibosheth and at that point he should have taken the opportunity to bring himself back to emotional and physical health, but he didn't. It seems that he lay around moaning over his fate and focusing on his problems. He'd allowed the fact that he'd been dropped to rule his life and paint his picture of himself; lameness had become the reason and excuse as to why he couldn't and wouldn't ever function effectively again.

He allowed his past to dictate his future, and it's so easy for us to do the same; yet it's vital that we make the choices not to do so. The way we allow ourselves to think, coupled with the things we focus on, have incredible strength to keep us in or lift us out of the bog that a victim mentality must immerse itself into in order to survive. Mephibosheth could have been like my Polish friend, who decided at 60 to get it right. That operation caused her a lot of pain, but the pain of healing was a good type of pain, far better than the crippled, broken walk she had had before.

To reach out and receive healing can be very painful, but it is far preferable to the life we will live otherwise. Jesus Christ called us to life, to freedom, to a straight walk, and a truthful lifestyle; but we have to be willing to go the distance to receive it.

So Christ has really set us free (Galatians 5:1a).

IMPRISONED BY THE PAST

So often we forget our calling to life and freedom, and instead, we live our lives in the prison of our past. There is no more tragic prisoner than the one who is captive in the place of freedom. There's a story often told about how elephants are trained as work animals. When they are young, they are shackled to a heavy pole by a large chain. No matter how much they pull and strain, they cannot get free. Eventually, they get used to being tethered and no longer attempt to get away. Over the years, the pole is replaced with something less strong and the chain is replaced by a rope. As a full grown animal, it would be easy to pull away and escape, but the elephant has grown so used to its captivity and so sure of its own inability to get free that it no longer attempts to get away.

There is no more tragic prisoner than the one who is captive in the place of freedom.

It's easy even for Christians to be like that elephant. There are times when we feel we've been so badly treated that we can never get over it. Something that happened in our family or our church or in our relationships was so traumatic that it seems to be beyond our capacity to receive healing, but Jesus knows what that is like. He was wounded in the house of His friends (see Zech. 13:6); His

*Forgiveness is
the power
to remember
without the
sting, which is
the only way
freedom comes.*

brothers didn't understand who He was and what He was doing, and He was consistently misunderstood and rejected because of the purpose of His life. He knows what we've gone through, and that's why He also knows that we can get free from it, regardless of how bad it was for any of us.

It's not a case of forgive and forget. If we forgot everything we forgave, we would have amnesia; there would be great gaps in our minds. Forgiveness is much more than that; it's the power to remember without the sting, which is the only way freedom comes. Forgiveness is the only way that the individual Christian (and therefore the Body of Christ) can gain the power to march forward in the purposes of God, no longer living out of rejection, disillusionment, or pain, but out of the triumph of the life of Christ who broke down the dividing walls we build around ourselves to keep from being hurt. One of life's greatest secrets is that we will be hurt, but Jesus made a way for us to live free from that hurt. I know that, because I have been dropped and become lame. At different times of my life and for different reasons (some of my own making), I have been wounded in the house of my family and friends, but I have also felt the energizing and strengthening power of Christ to forgive and go on to walk in total freedom, not bound by a victim mentality but living free by the grace of God.

Many people would rather live in lameness their whole lives rather than pay the cost of having the bones re-broken and reset in order to bring wholeness. It's painful to have to work it through, but God can restore us if we will make the choices to allow Him to.

He says, *"I will if you will!"* He says, *"I know you have been made lame, and you've been wounded in the house of your friends and family; but I have been there before you, and I have triumphed over the wounds, bringing life out of death."* The reason He died was for the lame, the brokenhearted, the failure, the confused, the ashamed; and the reason He lives is to restore to our strength, capacity and fullness in Him. No person or trauma has the right to take from us our freedom in Christ, or keep us from receiving the joy that is our strength. No force should be allowed to bring us down, never to rise again.

> *For the law of the Spirit of life in Christ Jesus has made me free from the law of sin and death* (Romans 8:2 NKJV).

In the same way that the law of aerodynamics overrules and supersedes the law of gravity, the law of the Spirit of life in Christ Jesus is able to overrule and supersede the law of sin and death, which is what captures us and keeps us lame. We've all been dropped, many of us many more times than we care to remember. We've all been deeply wounded in the house of our friends, in our family, in the church, in the very places where we expected to be safe; but there is a great triumph in being dropped and experiencing terrible lameness and then allowing the King of kings to restore you completely. He hates to do a partial job, but He will stop if we yell, "STOP!" It's not His intention that we be healed in a crushed position, but He won't make us accept the healing He wants to give; it has to be our choice to keep allowing Him to work on the damaged places, the places where pride and fear and confusion reign. The process of healing will initially cause pain as our attention is brought to

We've all been deeply wounded in the house of our friends, in our family, in the church, in the very places where we expected to be safe; but there is a great triumph in being dropped and experiencing terrible lameness and then allowing the King of kings to restore you completely.

the fact that we have a problem and then as we submit to the hands of the Great Physician who often has to re-break our brokenness in order to heal us straight, but it is so worth it.

Mephibosheth had to choose whether to receive partial or full restoration, and so do we. Jesus comes to us, not just to restore our property but to heal our crippled lifestyle so we can follow hard after Him. We are not called to be spiritually lame bystanders but living, breathing disciples who can keep pace with Him no matter where He goes.

The choice is ours alone. We can't do it by ourselves, but we are the only ones who can make the choice to do it.

CHAPTER SIX

How to Be a Ruler, Not an Eraser

*True heroism is remarkably sober, very un-dramatic. It is not
the urge to surpass others at whatever cost, but the urge to
serve others at whatever cost.*

Arthur Ashe

The issue of personal authority is highly relevant for a catalyst.
You can't be an influence for change without a level of authority operating in your life, regardless of your title or official position. The
Book of Proverbs addresses this issue when it says that a person
who can't rule himself is like a city that has no protection because
its walls are broken down (see Prov. 25:28). Authority must be personal before it can be anything else. Athletes must exercise authority over themselves during training times; otherwise they have no
chance of winning against any real competition. Students have to
make the hard choices to study rather than play, or they will pay the

Spiritual authority is given by God. We don't earn it per se, but we do have to receive it; and it is in the receiving that we find the work that needs to be done. Jesus gave His disciples authority and then actively trained them to exercise it.

consequences of a wasted year and a career that is less than what they would want.

Someone whose intention is to be used by God to change the world has to ask himself several key questions. Is spiritual authority any different from official authority? What is spiritual authority? Where do you get it? Is it handed to you along with a title and an official role, or is there something that must be done to acquire it? Why do some Christians clearly have authority and others don't?

Spiritual authority is given by God. We don't earn it per se, but we do have to receive it; and it is in the receiving that we find the work that needs to be done. Jesus gave His disciples authority and then actively trained them to exercise it.

And I have given you authority over all the power of the enemy, and you can walk among snakes and scorpions and crush them... (Luke 10:19).

He hand selected 72 people out from among the crowds who followed Him and sent them out to do what He alone had been doing, which was exercising spiritual authority in the spiritual realm. When they went, they found to their amazement that they were able to exercise the power He had given to them. Jesus didn't just give authority to those 72 people though; on the contrary, He has imparted His authority to all of us. However, we only have to take a look around the Church to see that we aren't all operating in it.

Our tendency is to think that those who operate in the type of ministry that exercises power over the enemy are special people

100

and that such a powerful ministry is not something everyday Christians can operate in. Yet this verse makes it clear that it was Jesus' full and deliberate intention that every Christian should walk in the kind of authority that He walked in. His intention was that His followers should function in a greater degree of the display of the power of God than He did (see John 14:12). But one of the major reasons that the hospitals in every nation are full and not empty is that the Church has not understood what it is to receive that authority. Jesus Christ said He has given us authority over all the power of the enemy; and as we glibly read that passage, we give mental assent to that idea, yet most Christians do not walk in that type of authority nor have most of the disciples of Jesus Christ down through the ages.

How did Jesus gain His authority? Where did He get it? He wasn't born exercising it, but rather at some point, He became a person of authority. Somewhere between His meeting with John the Baptist and the miracles that occurred from that time on, an event took place that made all the difference.

AFTER THE BAPTISM (LUKE 3:21-22)

Jesus met His cousin John by the Jordan and was baptized. Up until then, He'd been living a life of relative obscurity, but this event heralded the beginning of His public life and ministry. Immediately following the baptism, He was filled with Holy Spirit. What an awesome experience even for those who looked on as He came up out of the water and heard the audible voice of His Father telling the world that He was pleased with His Son. And then Holy Spirit joined the party and filled Him in a remarkable way.

My experience of being baptized in Holy Spirit was amazing, even though others may not have thought so or even noticed what was happening at the time. On the outside, things probably didn't appear to be all that different to those around me, but I was suddenly deeply aware of the presence of God in me. I had no idea what to do with Him, but I knew I was different and that I would never be the same again. God had begun a good work, and He has continued to be faithful to complete it in me (see 1 Thess. 5:24).

Chapter 4 of Luke finds Jesus performing amazing miracles and healing everyone who came to Him of every kind of disease. The people of His hometown were confused because until recently they'd known Him only as the carpenter's son and apprentice, and now He was operating in the supernatural as though He owned it! However, between the baptism and the miracles, there was a significant stage in His development.

In Luke 4:1-2, the very same Holy Spirit who filled Him with that amazing sense of God's power now *led* (some translations indicate the words "drove" or "thrust" would be more appropriate) Him into the wilderness, because Jesus had a special meeting to attend. He had an appointment with the devil and temptation. Imagine how we would feel if our personal assistant popped into the office to say, "Oh, by the way, you're next appointment is with the devil. He rang yesterday, and I slotted him in for this afternoon at three, right after your baptism."

PARADISE LOST

The reason that Jesus came to earth at all was because the authority given by God to man had been lost. God had bestowed authority on Adam and Eve in the Garden of Eden, and authority meant they had dominion, the right to rule over all the earth. To have something bestowed on you means you don't have to earn it; it's a gift. Adam and Eve's destiny was to rule, but when satan came to tempt Eve and won, the prize he took was the authority she and Adam had been given to rule the earth. When the devil had his appointment with Eve, he deceived her so that instead of being a ruler, she became an eraser. That's why the world is in a mess, and who of us can say that we would not do the same as that first couple did?

Rulership over the earth was intended to be a natural part of our character, attitude, and living standard; but the authority was lost not long after it was given. It wasn't lost through warfare and violence; it was lost through stealth and deception and temptation. The enemy is well aware of our weaknesses, and it is those things he works on in order to destroy our faith, or at the very least, prevent us from being effective.

EDEN ENDED (GENESIS 3:1-7)

Eve was tempted in three areas: the tree was good for food, pleasant to the eyes, and it was desirable to make her wise (see Gen. 3:6). In the New Testament, John refers to it as the lust of the flesh, the lust of the eyes, and the pride of life (see 1 John 2:16). Eve was offered the age-old temptations that we are offered; the difference was that this was the first time temptation was present in her frame of reference. It wasn't that she was presented with something she'd been longing for; the suggestion put to her was a completely new thought, yet just as enticing and seemingly valuable as temptation is to us still.

Because the authority was lost through deception and temptation, Jesus had to win it back on the same battleground. There was no point getting millions of angels to outnumber the enemy and get the authority back by sheer force; the battle had to be won on the same ground as it had been lost. For this reason, Jesus had to be tempted in the same areas that Eve had been tempted.

The interjection of doubt into the security Eve had lived in hitherto had been broken forever when the devil had hissed into her open heart the question, "Has God really said...?" Now he began the same way by questioning what Jesus had known to be the truth about who He was, but which had not yet been proven, maybe not even to Himself (see Luke 4:3-4). For 40 days, he followed Jesus through the desert, taking turns haranguing and sympathizing with Him. The devil stopped where He stopped, walked where He walked, and all the time, the sound of his voice came hissing through the silence, filling the emotional and mental space that Jesus had given over to the pursuit of God. The challenge came in the same three areas in which Eve had been attacked—physical desire, ownership, and pride. "I can see You're really hungry and You've been out here for a long time. If You really are the Son of God, why don't You just do a little miracle for Yourself? No one will know if You have something to eat before You get back. You can feed Yourself…You know You want to. If You really are who God says You are, it will be easy."

Jesus had chosen not to use physical force, but it's vital that we don't underestimate the power of the Sword of the Spirit, which is the Word of God (see Eph. 6:17). He used this weapon with devastating effect, dealing death to the enemy's suggestion with one blow. Again the enemy came, this time appealing to the avaricious desire that lies resident in all of us. He took Jesus up to a high mountain and showed Him everything He could have…if only He would switch allegiance and worship satan instead of God.

Do you know that worship and authority go together? Who we worship determines the where and how of our authority. Jesus understood that and wielded the Sword again, trouncing the enemy's strategy by speaking out the priorities of worship with such clarity that there was no room for denial. The only being in Heaven and earth that is worthy of our worship is our God. It has often been said that there is a God-shaped hole in every life, and no matter who or what we use to fill that place, it will remain unsatisfied, because that place is set apart for God alone and nothing else will fit. Often we try to fill that place with a person, or some obsession like extreme sports or family or career or image or even a cause, but the shape is all wrong; and no matter what our achievements, there are gaps throughout our soul that will not be satisfied. Worship of anything other than God is idolatry, no matter how pure or wholesome our focus may appear. We were created to worship God, and only that will satisfy the longing in our souls, whether we realize it or not.

To Eve the enemy had said, "Go on, eat it...it will make you wise." Eve already was wise! Her teacher was God. Every day they walked and talked together in the Garden. He told her everything she needed to know and the wisdom and intellect that she and Adam enjoyed was incredible; there was no other source of information that could have been given.

The only being in Heaven and earth that is worthy of our worship is our God. It has often been said that there is a God-shaped hole in every life, and no matter who or what we use to fill that place, it will remain unsatisfied, because that place is set apart for God alone and nothing else will fit.

However, there's something in us all that makes us draw to being better, stronger, wiser than someone else; and in succumbing to the desire for more than God would give her, she lost the battle, and with it went the authority and the dominion God had given them for nothing. She, and Adam as he followed suit, lost the right to rule over the earth. Instead of being a ruler, Eve became an eraser, and to this day, we still fight the same battle in the same three areas.

For the world offers only the lust for physical pleasure, the lust for everything we see, and pride in our possessions. These are not from the Father. They are from this evil world. And this world is fading away, along with every-thing it craves. But if you do the will of God, you will live forever (1 John 2:16-17).

Nothing is new; every sin we struggle with, every area we are tempted in is in one of those three areas. Physical lust is external. The issue could be sex, but it might not be. It could be food, alcohol, drugs, or addiction to adrenalin or success. The lust of the eyes relates to internal longings. There is always someone who has a better house, more money, fantastic holidays, or an amazing job or ministry. The craving for ownership is one of the most powerful forces to grip people's hearts in the last few centuries. We look to the right and the left, ceaselessly comparing ourselves with others. When we feel our efforts and what we produce are superior, a sense of satisfaction and well-being floods our hearts. But when we see that we have less than someone else, feelings of failure confront us with the notion that we therefore are less than them, and our frustration is exacerbated by the self-pity and resentment that sabotages all our efforts to improve.

Finally, satan appealed to an area which is so deeply entrenched in all of our hearts that we often don't realize it is there—the pride of life. He gave to Jesus the opportunity to prove in one fell swoop that He was truly God. Throwing Himself down from the temple, the place of worship which His own life personified, would have drawn all eyes to Him, and the worship that was due to Him would have instantly been given. No need for Gethsemane, no need for the cross; it was a shortcut that would eradicate the need for Him to suffer at all, in His quest to regain the authority.

Every battle Eve faced, every battle we face, Jesus Christ faced and won!

Every battle Eve faced, every battle we face, *Jesus Christ faced and won!* The Bible calls the devil the god of this world, because he won the authority from Eve. When Jesus went willingly with Holy Spirit into the wilderness to meet with the devil face-to-face, He was on a mission to win back the authority that had been lost to the human race eons ago in the Garden of Eden.

THE WAY OF THE WILDERNESS (ISAIAH 35)

The only way to gain the authority we've been given is by way of the wilderness. The ownership of authority doesn't come when the heavens open and Holy Spirit descends; that's just the beginning. To make the authority operable, we must be willing to journey via the wilderness, and it's in the wilderness that we lose or gain the authority that is given through the infilling of Holy Spirit.

The devil always tempts us in the place where we are weakest. If we feel we have little worth but we've been offered an amazing job that will make us important in the eyes of other people, although it will require that we compromise our values, the easiest thing to do is rationalize what we are doing…and take the job. Many people in ministry who I personally know were offered great jobs at the same time they were offered a ministry position. Often people who have made the decision to attend Bible College have suddenly been confronted with a promotion or the offer of a job they have always wanted; but of course, the price they would have to pay was no time to attend college. They had to make a choice between what would cause them to feel better about themselves in the eyes of their peers and what they believed that God was asking of them. A guy may have made the difficult choice to live for God in a life of purity and righteousness, and then along comes a really hot chick who really seems to like him. Someone may have decided to get involved with the children's ministry or street work, but suddenly there's a lot of overtime available at work that would make possible the purchase of a new plasma screen TV, simply by working weekends for the next three months.

TAKE A WALK ON THE WILD SIDE

Authority comes by way of the wilderness. After every great experience when God has met someone and infused them with a new level of His Holy Spirit, that new impartation must take time to be reinforced. New levels of spiritual authority can be set in stone only by our own choices, and we make these choices during the times we meet with the devil in the wilderness. When all is going well, it's comparatively easy to make right choices; but when problems abound, life seems dry and dusty, answers to prayer are few and far between, and we still make right choices, that's when we know that a new level of authority has been firmly locked in our hearts. Knowledge of the principles of God is not the same as walking by those principles.

When all is going well, it's comparatively easy to make right choices; but when problems abound, life seems dry and dusty, answers to prayer are few and far between, and we still make right choices, that's when we know that a new level of authority has been firmly locked in our hearts.

Jesus had so many opportunities to make His own answers fit His life, rather than to wait for God to supply in His timing. The first temptation that came to Him was hunger, and yet He was the Bread of God. Time in the wilderness is a hungry time; you don't feel as though you are being fed. All around there is a barrenness of hearing God; it's as though He has stopped listening and stopped speaking. The truth is, we have an appointment with the enemy, and the temptation that he offers is to turn our own stones into bread. It's so easy to find ways to feed yourself when God doesn't seem to be feeding you. Our time in the wilderness is designed to help us look at our own desires, up close and personal, because before we can walk in a new level of authority, we have to have the opportunity to reinforce whether what we believe is really true, or prove it all to be more than we are willing to live for. Like Jesus, we have the right to say "yes" to the enemy and turn our own stones into bread in order to keep from the hunger that overwhelms us, or to use the Sword of the Spirit that God has supplied to each of us to say, "No, I'm not going that way, no matter how much my longings are crying out for satisfaction. My choice is to live for God, and that is not negotiable."

Because He came to earth as man, all the temptations we feel, He felt also. Having the kingdoms of the world spread out before Him, along with the opportunity to demonstrate His right to be worshiped in one fell swoop must have touched the place in His heart which already understood the road ahead. Right then, at the beginning of His ministry, He had the opportunity to do for Himself and His call as Savior what only God should do. He chose to turn away from being His own Savior and allowed God to take Him via the road of greatest fruitfulness. It was after that time in the wilderness that the miracles began and the Kingdom of Heaven began to be received on earth!

It takes a few times of being driven/led/thrust by Holy Spirit out into the wilderness before we realize that we're actually meeting God there in a way that we never could at any other time or in any other place. Although our appointment is with the deceiver, if we choose to, we will find that we meet God in that barren place to a far greater extent than we ever dreamed possible. When someone gets used to that, they will find that the wilderness is no longer bare but beautiful, because of what they have allowed it to do in their life.

Our time in the wilderness is designed to help us look at our own desires, up close and personal, because before we can walk in a new level of authority, we have to have the opportunity to reinforce whether what we believe is really true, or prove it all to be more than we are willing to live for.

Everyone has a choice to make, the opportunity to decide to be a ruler or an eraser. Though Adam and Eve lost the authority that had been bestowed upon them, Jesus regained for us the right to have dominion in the spiritual realm. However, the choice is ours as to whether we will receive it personally and make the decision to diligently practice what is required, to cause what we've been given to embed itself into our lives and lifestyles, in order that it will not be just something we learned because others have told us, but a living, breathing, faithful authority that we live out every day. The wilderness looks like a place to be afraid of at the onset of our time there, but when that time is spent with Jesus Christ, Himself the Living Bread, we will gain the endurance to wait on Him and not try to meet our own needs in our own way.

CHAPTER SEVEN

The Man With the Ironclad Soul

In each age men of genius undertake the ascent. From below, the world follows them with their eyes. These men go up the mountain, enter the clouds, disappear, reappear; people watch them, mark them. They walk by the side of precipices. They daringly pursue their road. See them aloft, see them in the distance; they are but black specks. On they go. The road is uneven, its difficulties constant. At each step a wall, at each step a trap. As they rise the cold increases. They must make their ladder, cut the ice and walk on it, hewing the steps in haste. A storm is raging. Nevertheless they go forward in their madness. The air becomes difficult to breathe. The abyss yawns below them. Some fall. Others stop and retrace their steps; there is a sad weariness. The bold ones continue. They are eyed by the eagles; the lightning plays about them: the hurricane is furious. No matter, they persevere.

Victor Hugo

The Way Up Is Down

We've already covered one aspect of Joseph's life, but there is so much to learn from this man who allowed the events of his life to change not only him, but also the history of his people. Key to Joseph's story is a little known Scripture that can greatly enhance our understanding of how he was able to rise from the lowest of the low to the highest role in the land of Egypt.

Joseph's life was a series of highs and lows, but as with Jesus, the favor of God enabled him to win the favor of the people around him. Though he was promoted regularly, also just as regularly circumstances occurred that caused him to lose out, often through no fault of his own, forcing him to end up even lower than he was before. As a catalyst for change and as a potential leader of his people, it seemed his trajectory was all wrong—down instead of up!

Over a period of several years, he went from being the favorite son with the really cool coat to the pit and slave traders, to being the slave of Potiphar, to the jail and the jailer, and then suddenly and finally, to being the CEO of the nation. Those years were tough years of exile, misrepresentation, and being misunderstood, yet Joseph constantly gained respect and favor in every context of his life, whether high or low.

Perspective Is Everything (Genesis 45:1-8)

Finally the famine arrived and with it, Joseph's brothers. Through a frightening series of events, they were brought to the place where they stood before him now, suddenly aware of the awful truth. Looking at them in their weakened and helpless state, he remembered the last time he had related with them as their brother—the day they sold him to the slave traders. Violently they had dragged him out of the pit they'd just thrown him into; he pleaded in terror for his life, but they weren't listening. After all those years of resentment, hatred, and jealousy, their pent-up anger now exploded in an outburst of betrayal that changed the course of his entire life. The rejection of that day came again to his heart, and his eyes filled with tears at the memory of it.

Now the tables were turned, and Joseph had the upper hand. His dreams had come true, and here were his brothers, bowed before him. They were at his mercy just as he had been at theirs all those years ago. Now he could finally extract revenge on them for the way they had treated him then...but something had happened in him in the intervening years. Joseph now understood the bigger picture.

> But God sent me ahead of you to preserve for you a remnant on earth and to save your lives by a great deliverance. So then, it was not you who sent me here, but God. He made me father to Pharaoh, lord of his entire household and ruler of all Egypt (Genesis 45:7-8 NIV).

He was not resentful or angry, nor did he feel any need to make his brothers pay for their sin. Why? Because now he had God's perspective—he understood the One who is the Ultimate Recycler, able to take other people's cruelty, betrayal, and wrong actions to bring salvation and restoration. One of the key elements to being a visionary leader who is able to go the distance and not break down halfway through the process is this ability to see beyond personal hurt and pain to the bigger picture. It's this overarching quality of trust and faith in God that turns society's rejects into leaders of people and nations and provides the necessary stamina to go the distance, over whatever roads the journey will take them.

One of the key elements to being a visionary leader who is able to go the distance and not break down halfway through the process is this ability to see beyond personal hurt and pain to the bigger picture.

How is God able to do that? How would you respond if you were Joseph? If the tree that represents your life was planted, what fruit would it produce? Would it be the fruit of the deliberate choices to forgive and keep loving because Jesus Christ has been allowed to work in your life to transform pain into purpose and peace; or would it be the shrivelled, bitter fruit of rejection and vengeance, justified through and because of your suffering? What was the process that took Joseph through those long years where rejection and betrayal was his closest and most constant companion?

AN IRON COLLAR AND CUFFS

Then He sent someone to Egypt ahead of them—Joseph, who was sold as a slave. There in prison, they bruised his feet with fetters and placed his neck in an iron collar. Until the time came to fulfill his word, the Lord tested Joseph's character. Then Pharaoh sent for him and set him free; the ruler of the nation opened his prison door. Joseph was put in charge of all the king's household; he became ruler over all the king's possessions (Psalm 105:17-21).

It's clear from this psalm that God was obviously in charge of Joseph's situation. The Amplified Bible translation makes the process Joseph went through even clearer. He was shackled by iron, but amazingly, he gradually came to a place where his soul entered into that iron while he was being refined like metal to become the leader God designed him to be. It was after his soul entered into the iron that he became ruler of the people.

*His feet they hurt with fetters; he was laid in chains of iron and **his soul entered into the iron**. Until his word [to his cruel brothers] came true, until the word of the Lord tried and tested him (Psalm 105:18-19 AMP, emphasis added).*

Joseph told his brothers that it was really God who had *sent* him ahead of them to preserve their lives. The word *sent* means "to appoint" or "to sow." God appointed Joseph right from the time of his birth; he was literally *sown* into the situation in Egypt so that he would grow into the leader his dreams had foretold to him. Until the time came for the prophetic dreams to be fulfilled, his character was tested over and over in many painful ways.

For anyone who has dreams from God about making a difference with their life, this is one of the most relevant lessons a person can learn. Until such time that our character becomes what it needs to be in order to do the task we are appointed to, our capacity to be a catalyst for the purposes of God will be tested repeatedly in a multitude of curious but common ways. Rejection will come from the most unexpected quarters; opportunities for bitterness and disillusionment will be presented at every turn giving us the opportunity to keep going back to God in our pain, choosing to receive healing from Him in the places where we have been devastated.

If that doesn't happen and we find a way to sidestep the dealings of God by hardening our hearts or retreating from the source of suffering, when the time comes to make a difference we will not be able to operate in the way God had in mind when He initially sowed us into that situation. It is so easy, when we know the call of God on our lives but are not seeing it come to pass, to get

It was after his soul had entered into the iron that he became ruler of the people.

uptight about what isn't happening; but the key is to realize that it's the "what isn't" in our circumstances that is preparing us for the "what will be."

I became a Christian after I was married, and for the first seven years after that, my husband was not a Christian. The wives of non-Christian husbands in the church I went to often spent time together, and the general feeling that used to come out of those times was that because of our situation we could not effectively serve the Lord. God had to intervene in my life to show me that the way forward for me, as for everyone in any situation, is to serve where you are. Faithfulness with what you have, however little and unnoticed, will give Him free access to your life so that, should He choose, He can give you more opportunities to be faithful. Nothing is too small or too insignificant for God to notice us doing. My years operating the overhead projector and looking after the children in the crèche when others seemed to be doing more enjoyable jobs in the church have more than reaped their reward in the way God has chosen to use me as the years have gone on. Those times were not easy, but my soul found a way to enter into the iron rather than allow my heart to be hardened by what appeared not to be, and God found a way to use me because of it.

A CATALYTIC CONVERTER

The amazing thing is that the success or failure of our role as a catalyst for the purposes of God always pivots on our choices. We have observed people who were serving with great strength in the Body of Christ as leaders and role models, and then suddenly...they disappeared. What happened? Sometimes it's just that they got sick and tired of being tested; they'd had enough. Regardless of how right and good we appear on the surface, in each one of us are hidden flaws that are not visible initially but will, at times, be suddenly exposed to deeper levels of testing. The first reason for this testing is to expose to our hearts our own sad inadequacy and to show us again how deeply we need Jesus Christ to cleanse us and make us what we should be. Secondly, once exposed to ourselves, we are able to bring our issues into the light for the purposes of getting rid of them. It's at this point that many falter and fall, because the greater the measure of credibility that has been established through a catalyst's life, the more humiliating it is for them to acknowledge to those around them that they have a problem. It's on this hurdle that most disgraced ministries have been brought down.

Joseph was tested through his brothers' rejection and betrayal; he was tested by lust and intimidation; he was tested by injustice; and rejection again when he was used by the butler and then forgotten. Through all of those things, and a multitude more humiliating and soul destroying events that happened to him as a slave, which are not written down, he continued to deal with his heart, forgiving and repenting and staying focused on his relationship with the One who had spoken to him in his dreams all those years before, when it had all seemed possible.

Above all else, guard your heart, for it affects everything you do (Proverbs 4:23).

Our lives are filled with pressure and problems, each one seemingly designed to keep us from God's intention that our life be a catalyst for His purposes, yet these things actually aren't intended to stop us from reaching our destiny. Rather, they are the means by which God trains and equips us for the tasks ahead of us. It's imperative that we remain aware of this process so that it is not short-circuited. The person who can find a shortcut will never become the catalyst for breakthrough he was designed to be, because regardless of how enticing the shortcut appears to be and how much it looks as though it is going where we want to go, it will never actually lead us to our destination.

The pivot point of Joseph's success in leadership is found in verse 18 (AMP): *"His feet they hurt with fetters; he was laid in chains of iron and his soul entered into the iron."* How does that translate for 21st-century Christians? Literally, it means there came a time when Joseph stopped struggling against the tools God had chosen to shape him. He not only stopped struggling against the iron chains, but more importantly, his soul made the choice to *enter into the iron.* It's vital to note that this didn't mean that Joseph gave up and stoically chose *que sera sera* (whatever will be, will be) as the preferred method of coping with the pain, as so many Christians do. Hard situations and the drudgery of continually making right choices with seemingly no success often results in feeling that believing God's word is just too difficult. It seems much easier to opt for the safety of not believing for anything but simply get through life trying to dull the pain of rejection, betrayal, and failure. This choice is a non-choice! The person who makes this choice makes the decision to live at a lesser level than they are called to.

Our soul and spirit often fight for mastery of our body because whatever rules our body rules our life.

They will certainly find their place in Heaven, but their lives will not be lived in the triumph of fulfilling their destiny.

Without a doubt, when we are attempting to usher in the Kingdom of God, it's our own souls that give us the most trouble. We are made in the image of God, and like Him, we are a triune being consisting of spirit, soul, and body (see 1 Thess. 5:23). Our body is just the tent, the vehicle to get us around; our spirit is that part of ourselves that is able to have direct communication with Him because we are made in His image. Like Him, we are essentially spiritual beings having a physical experience, as someone once said. Our soul is a complex mixture of mind, will, and emotions; and this is the part of us that wants to take charge of our lives because it is our spirit, the aspect of us that has free access to God, which should dictate who we are according to the plan of God. Our soul and spirit often fight for mastery of our body because whatever rules our body rules our life. Our soul uses its energy justifying our sin, our unforgiveness, our bitterness, and pride and resentment, our fear and rejection and selfishness. It is our soul that tells us we have a right to feel and act the way we do; and if it's allowed to, our soul will abort our call and prevent us from reaching our destiny as a catalyst for God's purposes.

For God to have His way in our life, our soul has to make the choice to cooperate with Him in whatever ways He chooses to test us. In Joseph's times of pain and confusion when he was shackled with iron chains, his soul made the amazing but powerful choice to enter into the iron. He learned to work with his suffering, embracing it rather than running from it, much like a woman in labor helps herself if she works with the contractions that are bringing her baby to birth rather than fighting against them. Every person who wants God to use his or her life must make the choice to allow Holy Spirit to take them, as He did Jesus, into the place where fears, temptations, doubts, and suffering abound, because it's only in that place that God can show us who we really are and who we can be if we do it His way. It's not a place to be afraid of; He gives angels to watch over us while He's at work in our hearts (see Ps. 91:11-12).

That's why Paul and Silas were able to sing while fettered by their iron chains in a jail, their blood still dripping on the floor from the whipping they'd taken earlier in the day. They were not grumbling and complaining, or traumatized by their experience; they were using the circumstances they were going through as part of their expression of faith in a God who loves and cares for them. And amazingly, it was this singing that caused the earthquake that not only set

In Joseph's times of pain and confusion when he was shackled with iron chains, his soul made the amazing but powerful choice to enter into the iron. He learned to work with his suffering, embracing it rather than running from it.

them free, but enabled the jailer and his whole household to be saved.

Paul and Silas understood what it was to be chained. Their souls were already trained by other experiences of hardship and suffering to make the choice to enter into the iron. That's why Paul's legacy still serves us today, and he continues to teach us how to live as a catalyst for Jesus Christ. In the same way that Joseph's journey saved his nation, Paul's shipwrecks and beatings, his imprisonments and times in the wilderness made him into the man who could write to you and me, advising us how to be better Christians…and his advice still works.

If Not Us, Then Who? If Not Now, Then When?

Joseph began with a dream; it was a call to leadership. In his immaturity he didn't understand what the road to becoming the leader God intended him to be would cost him. He ended with a bigger picture, and in the process he came to understand that it was not all about him and that there were bigger things at stake than his own comfort and security. The call of God wasn't all about Joseph, even though in the beginning he thought it was. It was about the salvation of a nation, and everything that happened to him was for the purpose of bringing deliverance to that nation.

Each of us is called to a nation. We're called to intentionally cross the boundaries that separate us from the people who don't know who Jesus is. We've been sown into whatever nation we live in so that we can help its people understand what is happening and how to deal with it. We've been appointed to be catalysts for the purposes of God, right here, right now. What that will take is the laying down of our lives, our dreams for ourselves, and our personal ambition in order to take up the purposes of God. It's about making our own choices not to be helpless victims of the chains of iron that weigh us down, but to turn the tables on our enemy and make the choice to enter into that iron with the grace of God. It is these choices that bring endurance to our walk, enabling us to go the whole distance. Someone once said that Christians should have tough feet and a tender heart, but it takes the wilderness to make that happen, because we start out with the opposite.

At first our hearts are too tough to feel the pain and heartache of the people God wants to sow us among, and our feet are too soft and tender to go there, even if we wanted to. We want to protect ourselves from pain; after all, we've already had enough pain and we would like to avoid it at all costs. The problem is, only one thing can be tough at a time in the life of a Christian—either the heart or the feet. The testing is what breeds tenacity into our lives, as well as the capacity to feel the pain of others and treat them with compassion instead of seeking revenge or ownership of them. It's the testing that forms in us the willingness to allow Him to do whatever is necessary to enable His plans for our lives and our nations to come to pass.

Each one of us is called, like Joseph, to be a catalyst to save the people God has sown us among. He has sent us out ahead of them so that by the time they experience the issues that we have faced, be it death or divorce, hardship, abuse or rejection, we will be able to show them that it is possible to turn all the damage around and use it as manure to grow a good life with. That's impossible without God at work, but if He is there in us, they will see His power to change their lives.

We've been sown into whatever nation we live in so that we can help its people understand what is happening and how to deal with it.

CHAPTER EIGHT

Mirror, Mirror on the Wall

And do not compare yourself with others or you will become vain and bitter.

Desiderata

One of the greatest self-inflicted sources of pain we can experience is our suicidal tendency to compare ourselves with other people. Wherever we look we cannot help but evaluate how much better or worse we are than others who share our context for living. Friends, family, neighbors…no one escapes the often unconscious scrutiny that springs from our never ending search for personal worth that we attempt to find in the face of how well we are doing compared to everyone else.

Though we know and may even easily quote the words that assure us that God has a plan for our lives (see Jer. 29:11), the degree to which we believe it is shown by the level of chagrin we feel when someone else gets something we feel we should be able to have…even if we didn't actually want it until we knew they had it. Life loses its richness so often in the face of, not personal failure, but the failure to be seen as the top turkey on our own personal hill.

This problem is as ancient as mankind, and yet the choices we make to put aside our own desires in order to serve God's purposes include the necessity to stop our endless comparisons of ourselves with everyone else.

IMAGE—EGAMI

The bronze washbasin and its bronze pedestal were cast from bronze mirrors donated by the women who served at the entrance of the Tabernacle (Exodus 38:8).

The chapters surrounding this verse are all about the building of the tabernacle. It was a portable work of art, built exactly according to God's instructions; but in the middle of the description of what it looked like, this little verse seems to pop up almost irrelevantly. Nowhere else in the entire project are we specifically told what something had been before it was used in the temple!

Reading this, a number of questions spring to mind. Why does it matter what the brazen laver was made of? What does bronze signify? What did the women who served at the temple do? They must have needed to look presentable for their job, but how would they know they did if they'd given all their mirrors away? There's nothing written about this job, and the only other mention of it is in the Book of Samuel where we are told that Eli's sons were seducing the women serving at the entrance to the tabernacle (see 1 Sam. 2:22). Considering the distance of years between these two accounts, it is clear that whatever their role was, it was an ongoing ministry function.

Most people in church life do not have a title, but all of us are called to minister at the entrance to the temple. In the Old Testament this was a place, but under the New Covenant, which was signed, sealed, and delivered by the death and resurrection of Jesus Christ, those who love Jesus Christ have become the temple (see 1 Cor. 3:16). Incredibly, that means that each individual Christian is a temple. Therefore, the smallest ministry to someone else, even if it's merely buying them a coffee or talking them through relationship issues and encouraging them to try again when they've been disappointed, is serving at the entrance to their temple. If they are now the temple of the Holy Spirit, the implication is that whenever we help others to facilitate their lives and ministry, whether it's by organizing an event, praying for them or counselling them, teaching them more about Jesus Christ, or fixing their car or computer, we are ministering at the entrance to their temple, which literally means we serve at the entrance to other people's relationship with Jesus. Even if they do not know Him as their Savior, what we do for them is something that can facilitate their journey towards Him.

The reason that there is no job description for these women is because each of us is uniquely designed to serve Him in different ways. If there was a job description entailed in this role, we'd automatically go into judgment mode, which categorizes people's value by what they do, and we would affirm or despise ourselves or others based on whether we fit the description of the role. The truth is, when a person is doing what they're called to do for you, they are serving at the entrance to your temple, and the reverse is also true.

However, the ministry of serving in the context of the Church is curious because, as in so many other areas, it so easily gets mixed up with our picture of ourselves. Someone said to me once, "Wouldn't it be interesting to see just for one day, how everyone else sees you?" It might be good…or it may be disastrous, because

What makes us feel better about ourselves isn't easily defined because it's to do with our perspective on life, which is made up of intangibles, including our world view and the values of the people in our circle of relationship.

people don't always see us the way we want to be seen, nor do they even see us as we truly are.

We so easily base our value on external things, such as the fact that everyone likes the person we are married to, or worse, they don't! We may feel less valued because we're not married at all. A degree from a top university instead of the local technical college might be enough to help us feel superior, or the fact that we live in a bigger house or have a much larger salary, or we're invited to other places to preach.

What makes us feel better about ourselves isn't easily defined because it's to do with our perspective on life, which is made up of intangibles, including our world view and the values of the people in our circle of relationship. For instance, if they don't place value on money and prestige, they won't be impressed by the house and the yacht. If it's conservation and radical action they are into, they will be more impressed because you chained yourself to a tree in a rain forest for six months and got arrested for doing it.

When a person is driven by the need to feel important, special, as good or better than other people, the result is that they find themselves doing things they would not normally do and acting in a way they would not choose to act of their own volition; and they do it all to impress the people they are with and gain their acceptance. It's a broken world, and people fake all sorts of attitudes and philosophies in order to get other people's attention and favor.

ALL THINGS NEW?

Change is supposed to happen when a person becomes a Christian. We've been told that God loves us for who we are, not for what we do. We're taught that His favor comes as an inherent part of our relationship with Him; and yet, even though we know it's true, it often takes some time to really understand and believe that, and some Christians never do. God says He loves each of us equally, but there are times we find that a little hard to believe. It's easy to think that He loves the student who gets straight A's better than the one who struggles to finish her exams. We're sure He must love the person who's at church 24/7 better than the one who drops by every few weeks, and often we are convinced that the pastor and God have a private line not available to the rest of us.

Regardless of our inner opinions that some people are more special to God than others, which would explain why they have more resources at their disposal, the Bible says that God gifts us according to the tasks He's assigned to us, rather than out of any sense of preference of one above another.

> *What makes you better than anyone else? What do you have that God hasn't given you? And if all you have is from God, why boast as though you have accomplished something on your own?* (1 Corinthians 4:7)

There's nothing that we have that wasn't given to us freely in order to get done what He has called us to do. He intentionally designed us for specific purposes (see Eph. 2:10). That's why it's not only so futile to envy each other the circumstances of our lives but also ridiculous to try to impress each other, even if we can. The way we impress only lasts for this lifetime, but while we're trying to get each other's favor, we're wasting time we could have used doing what God wants.

So much of what we do is based on what we hope people will think of us. We posture ourselves, posing to impress others because we are so concerned about what other people think. This is where the mirrors of the serving women in the temple become relevant to us in the 21st century.

CHECK IT OUT

The purpose of the bronze laver was for cleansing the priests. The bowl that was filled with water stood between the tabernacle and the altar. Each time the priests went past the altar and into the tabernacle, they were to stop and wash their hands and feet in the basin (see Exod. 40:30-32). Water always represents the Word of God (see Eph. 5:26), and this verse correlates with Paul's instructions to us that if we will examine ourselves, we will not have to be examined by God (see 1 Cor. 11:31). As the priests walked past the altar, which represents the sacrifice of Jesus Christ, and into the presence of God, they looked into the water and symbolically washed those parts of their body that would have been defiled by the ordinary events of their ministry. Literally, they judged themselves so they would not be judged by God when they went into His presence. It is God's intention that we examine ourselves by His Word and not by other people's opinions. The hands of the priests represented their ministry; their feet represented their own personal walk with God. The need for the mirror was not to check out how they appeared to others, but to show them what needed cleansing in their day-to-day life. Regardless of our role or ministry position, we all need to do that.

It is God's intention that we examine ourselves by His Word and not by other people's opinions.

Biblically, *bronze* always symbolizes judgment, but if you've ever looked into a bronze plate, you will know that it is difficult to judge your appearance by it; it is not a very clear reflector. No matter how expensive the plate or how highly polished it is, the reflection is still warped, and you can't get a true picture.

Fear of man causes us to lose characteristics of ourselves, parts of our personhood that are unique.

When we judge ourselves by each other and try to modify our behavior to impress other people, we are modeling our inner life on everyone else's standards, and that causes horrendous damage to who we really are. Trying to do this is really the fear of man, which the Bible says is like a steel trap (see Prov. 29:25) that grabs you with cruel teeth and won't let you go free without losing something of yourself. In countries where animals are trapped, it is horribly common for an animal like a fox to gnaw off its own leg in order to get free, even though the result will still be death. Fear of man causes us to lose characteristics of ourselves, parts of our personhood that are unique. Valuable aspects of our lives die because our desire to win the approval of other people means that we jettison aspects of ourselves that make us who we are, in order to look like something we think would make us more acceptable to others. All of this relates to the bronze mirror—examining ourselves using judgment that is warped and lacking the ability to give a true picture.

That's why the serving women gave their mirrors away. In their desire to contribute to the establishment of the house of God, something changed in their hearts, and they came to understand that however good they looked to other people, it wouldn't mean anything if God didn't approve. Giving up their mirrors meant they were now relying on God to show them who they were and what they should look like.

God's favor has nothing to do with what onlookers see; it's about the heart. When God sent Samuel to find the king whom He had chosen, He told Samuel that it was imperative not to be fooled by how the person looked. That's how Samuel ended up choosing someone no one ever thought of as a leader to take the greatest role in the nation and become one of the greatest kings in history.

VOTED LEAST LIKELY

Is that you? How many of us are the person our friends and enemies and families would have voted least likely to be a catalyst for God? Not all that gifted, no great abilities, pretty extreme character, or not all that significant…and yet God is using you or calling you into leadership. It's vital that we gain the revelation that it's not other people who are responsible for how we serve God; it is God who will raise us up. It's His favor we need! When we have His favor, the favor of people generally follows, as it did with Jesus. (Mind you, He got crucified as well….)

When you position yourself, make sure it's toward God and not people. When Lot went out to the land Abram gave him, he positioned himself toward the big town of Sodom (see Gen. 13:12), even though he knew it was a corrupt place, and before long he ended up living there (see Gen. 14:12). Don't position yourself to impress people or be comfortable; position yourself to please God.

THE MIRROR EFFECT

But we all, with unveiled face beholding as in a mirror the glory of the Lord, are being transformed into the same image from glory to glory, just as from the Lord, the Spirit (2 Corinthians 3:18 NASB).

When we get rid of our own evaluations about ourselves that have been framed by the warped ideals of our society in favor of wanting to know God's opinion, everything about the way we see ourselves begins to change. The word "transformed" in the

Scripture above literally means "metamorphosis"; we change from one thing into another. Our old attitudes and habits and motivations, when faced with the glory of God, morph into new attitudes and actions so that our heart becomes increasingly like the heart of God.

> *...keeping our eyes on Jesus, on whom our faith depends from start to finish (Hebrews 12:2a).*

No matter how great another person is, he or she can never be the author of my salvation! Everyone deserves dignity and respect, and the Bible says that those who work to teach us God's Word are worthy of double honor (see 1 Tim. 5:17). Despite this, if we allow the role of those we love and follow to get out of perspective, we will be deeply disillusioned when they show themselves to be merely human. Don't damage your relationship with God or your leaders by confusing which is which.

If we allow the role of those we love and follow to get out of perspective, we will be deeply disillusioned when they show themselves to be merely human.

> *And remember, it's a message to obey, not just listen to. For if you listen and don't obey, it is like looking at your face in a mirror but doing nothing to improve your appearance. You see yourself, walk away, and forget what you look like. But if you keep looking steadily into God's perfect law—the law that sets you free—and if you do what it says and don't forget what you heard, then God will bless you for doing it (James 1:22-25).*

If we choose to make the Word of God our mirror, rather than other people's opinions, we will be set free from the need to perform in order to gain approval, and our effectiveness will increase hugely.

Ultimately, reaching our destiny in Christ is not about how we look to other people, no matter how much we respect them. Even though it's a biblical principle to honor those who serve us as leaders and pour their lives into helping us become who God has called us to be, those people are not God. If they hold a wrong place in your life and then disappoint you, it will rock your faith, because your faith has been fixed on them rather than on Jesus. When a person looks for the favor of people more than the favor of God, even unknowingly, they walk in the fear of man, which brings the judgment that the bronze symbolizes. When those serving women clung to their mirrors, they reserved the right to judge for themselves how well they were doing, how they appeared, who was noticing, whether or not they had the approval and admiration of the people around them.

Giving up their mirrors literally symbolizes to us giving up the fear of man. The mirrors were laid down as a sacrifice to God; and because God is the ultimate recycler of the inadequacies we surrender to Him, those mirrors were used for a much greater purpose, being transformed, that is, undergoing metamorphosis to become the vehicle by which God alone can judge the heart and wash away the mucky residue that sometimes lodges there. We are to follow the example of the Old Testament priests each day as we come into the presence of God through the sacrifice of Jesus. We need to look into the Word of God, checking the state of our heart, our motives, and our intentions in order to receive forgiveness for anything that is what it shouldn't be, and to ensure that nothing in our hearts is blocking our prayers from being answered (see Ps. 66:18). If God is happy with us, generally the rest will follow, because in the Kingdom of God, our motivation dictates our effectiveness.

In the Kingdom of God, our motivation dictates our effectiveness.

DO IT YOURSELF

If the Church is to succeed in its mandate to change the world, something has to change about how we look at ourselves, what we judge ourselves by, and how we measure our worth! It's been many years since the Lord first spoke to me about these mirrors, and I made the decision to surrender my warped, unclear, dysfunctional, rebellious mirror of judgment and performance orientation to the purposes of God. I decided that I would judge myself only according to what God says, not what my peers are saying, not what my history dictates, and not what my ambitions try to push me to be and do. That doesn't mean I'm not teachable, because I do value and appreciate the ministry of those I look to for leadership; but it does mean that I do not put those people in the place of God. That decision has been challenged often, and I haven't always passed the test; but God continues to work in me to accomplish this.

Transparency means that I am able to repent when I would rather justify myself; that I am able to forgive when I want to reject someone who has hurt me or who doesn't live up to my expectations.

Living this way has meant being transparent, even though transparency has cost me dearly at times and has been used as a weapon against me. However, I have maintained my determination to continue to be transparent, regardless of the consequences, because when I'm wrong, it serves God's purposes better if I quickly realize and acknowledge it; and if I'm right, He has promised to vindicate me (see Isa. 54:17). Transparency means that I am able to repent when I would rather justify myself; that I am able to forgive when I want to reject someone who has hurt me or who doesn't live up to my expectations. It means that when I catch myself thinking wrongly, I can deliberately and with intentionality chase those thoughts through to see what's really hidden behind what I'm thinking, and it gives me room to repent for a wrong heart. Do I always do this? No, I don't, but I'm working toward it; and I'm a lot further along than I used to be.

THE SEDUCTION OF RELIGION

This last point is highly relevant for church life. Samuel makes reference to a season when Eli's corrupt sons were seducing some of the women who served at the entrance to the temple (see 1 Sam. 2:22). Their role as priests serves to indicate what can happen even in the house of God; and even though morality may be the issue here, this point is even more relevant when we see the sort of seduction of the heart that can take place even among good and godly people.

It is too easy for any of us to begin ministering out of nothing else but a servant heart and end up being seduced by the spirit of religion into legalism, pride, rebellion, and lack of accountability, as well as by the need to be someone else's savior, or trying to make them be yours. Instead, we should simply take our place at the entrance to another's temple, serving others in whatever way God has gifted us in order to facilitate their relationship with Him and allow them to do the same for us. This is an incalculably precious opportunity to help them see Jesus at work more clearly than they could have done otherwise.

As a good friend of mine has written on her emails, "The heart of the matter is the matter of the heart."

HAND ME YOUR LOOKING GLASS

As I stood peering at the image reflected in the glass,
Thinking about what pleased me.
A check in my spirit made me avert my eyes
And turn the glass face down...

Then, with the world shut out, I sensed
That I now viewed the image reflected in my Father's eyes.

The image there bore no relation to the image
I had seen in the glass,
And suddenly, losing the imitation seemed no loss…
And I handed Him the glass!

Sheila Boakes

CHAPTER NINE

The View From Above

...for you are a chosen people. You are a kingdom of priests,
God's holy nation, His very own possession. This is so you
can show others the goodness of God, for He called you out
of the darkness into His wonderful light. Once you were not
a people; now you are the people of God... (1 Peter 2:9-10).

The Church tends to cop a lot of flack, even from Christians. Accusations broadly span issues of hypocrisy, lack of love, lack of vision, lack of faith, lack of good teaching, and lack of life; and it is on the basis of these flaws that many people who love Jesus Christ become disappointed and disillusioned and make the decision to abandon their church in favor of living a singular Christian life, whatever that may look like.

In spite of that, there is no question that the Church is the vehicle God has chosen to implement His plan for the world; and although

There is no Plan B!

He can and does use anyone to bring about His purposes, it is the Church as His collective people who operate as His ambassadors in every nation. There is no Plan B! Whatever the Church chooses or refuses to do in its representation of Jesus Christ is what society sees as God at work...or not, as the case may be. As the Bride of Christ, it is Jesus' intention that the Church be the instrument for His grace and mercy to operate among every people group. The Church stands unchallenged as the capital of the Kingdom of God, embodying as it obeys Jesus' mandate to govern the spiritual realm in whatever context it finds itself.

CHURCH—THE HOPE OF THE WORLD?

As a people, the Church is an incredible and unique entity. It is made up of people of every race and culture who have come to the awesome revelation that Jesus Christ died and rose again to redeem them from their own sin and out of their racial and cultural classifications. These people combine together in a unique and powerful union known as the Church (see Rev. 5:9-10). Regardless of individual preferences, perspectives, biases, and backgrounds, when the Church goes to meet Jesus in the air, it will be altogether (see 1 Thess. 4:16-17). There will be no separate categories, no divisions, or elite classifications according to denomination or rank; all of us will be one in Christ (see Col. 3:11,15).

That's God's view, but it isn't always the way we see it. Sad to say, the Church has at times earned its reputation of corruption, hypocrisy, pride, and prejudice, preferring traditions and fame, pomp and ceremony to an open, honest, and loving relationship with God, His people, and His world.

So now I am giving you a new commandment: Love each other. Just as I have loved you, you should love each other.

138

Your love for one another will prove to the world that you are My disciples (John 13:34-35).

We haven't had a great deal of success in demonstrating this Scripture. The world hasn't always equated the Church with the claims of Christ. Many people who have no problem with Jesus wouldn't darken the door of a church for fear of the disapproval and condemnation they would meet, and often they are correct. Even more sadly, the Church is finding that Christians are also voting with their feet. Over recent years, unprecedented numbers of jaded and cynical Christians have made the decision that church is not for them, feeling they can worship God better at home alone or with a handful of like-minded friends.

It's true that God can be worshiped anywhere and everywhere, because worship is a state of the heart, as opposed to being certain holy songs we sing in a certain holy building. However, in the same way, Church is a body of people, which means that making the decision to stop meeting together with other believers can never mean we have ceased to be part of the Church. Someone once said that when a Christian points an accusing finger at the Church, they are pointing three fingers back at themselves. That's because every Christian is a part of the Church, whether they want to be or not. It's true that the Church is full of hypocrites, but that was Paul's point when he said that he did things he didn't want to do and then he didn't do what he should do (see Rom. 7:14-25). Lamenting his own wretchedness, he went on to talk about Jesus Christ being the only avenue for him to escape from his body, which was overwhelmed with sin and death. It's remarkable and somewhat encouraging to realize that Paul, the person who has possibly influenced the Christian world more than any other except Jesus, struggled with the same issues that we do. The difference between him and many Christians is that Paul was willing to acknowledge his own issues in his situation rather than attempt to shift the blame and make everyone else responsible for his failure to be what he ought to be. In other words, he didn't abandon ship...and therein lies a great secret to an effective church life.

When a Christian withdraws from Church, citing the faults of other church members as their justification, they are unknowingly absenting themselves from God's plan and their place in it. This plan is that the Church is the hope of the world, as Bill Hybels so passionately puts it. Our mandate is to make disciples of every nation, baptizing them and teaching them about Jesus and His power to bring freedom (see Matt. 28:18-20). It's very clear and quite simple really; the difficulties lie in the doing of it. Nevertheless, as we focus on Him and develop a vision for what He intends rather than on what others are or are not doing, it becomes easier to believe that He wants to use us despite our inadequacies and imperfections.

The difference between him and many Christians is that Paul was willing to acknowledge his own issues in his situation rather than attempt to shift the blame and make everyone else responsible for his failure to be what he ought to be.

It is true that at times a particular church may have lost its way, and members may no longer be able to identify with the way it is representing Jesus to its environment. However, making the choice to leave Church altogether is a drastic and unfruitful way of handling the situation. No church is perfect, but if you feel you no longer fit in the church you are in, there is always another church, if you will take the time to ask God where your future lies. At times we become so entrenched in a certain tradition of worship or the sense of family we have found through a long period of time in a church we have loved but which has now lost its vision, that it seems impossible to change. Grieving because no other church is the same, we focus on the things that are different to what we are used to, and feel we can't bear the intense emotional and spiritual pressure required to go through the whole process of becoming part of a new way of "being" church. It is often at this point that people make the choice to cut and run—to stay at home and worship God there. This is a major mistake that will not only short-circuit many of the things that God wants to use you for, but will also cause your spiritual growth to be stunted because of your refusal to walk with Him through the important maturing experiences you can have at times like this.

God's call is not confined to one type of person or church; every church and Christian in the world has the same mandate, but the outworking of the call is unique to each of us as individuals and also to each church in every district and nation. God at times uses periods of dissatisfaction to take us out of places where we may have been content but our faith has grown stale. Despite our bewilderment, He knows that in a new environment we can be challenged again to grow and take on new roles and responsibilities we may otherwise never have thought of. It's entirely likely that people would never leave their old church had unhappiness not prodded them to it. In the same way that Paul and Barnabas formed a successful two-pronged mission into the world because of the conflict they experienced over John Mark (see Acts 15:36-41), we also at times fail to hear the voice of God until He allows things to become so uncomfortable that we are finally willing to change. However, forsaking Church altogether is not the answer, but often finding a new church is exactly what God is aiming at. This doesn't mean that we move from church to church never settling anywhere, but it does mean that there are times when God is calling us to a new thing; and we need to have ears to hear, no matter how comfortable we have been where we are.

Being a "called-out" people, handpicked for the task, may at times mean leaving one place to go to another as God does His amazing chess moves that bring the right people together at the right time in order to do the right thing. That's why church-growth programs when replicated across the nations, rarely have the same amazing success that they have in their place of origin.

We would prefer to purchase a packet of "Church Growth Principles," add water, and shake.

This is because each place is different, and each people are distinct, which means that our innate desire to package and franchise church growth is continually frustrated by the fact that God wants us to find out from Him how He wants to run our particular church and who should be there for what reason. We would prefer to purchase a packet of "Church Growth Principles," add water, and shake.

It's too easy for any of us to take potshots at the Church, distancing ourselves from those around us because of our inability to identify with why they do what they do. The mainline churches strike at the Charismatics and Pentecostals, who respond by condemnation of an equally damaging variety. The Protestants and Catholics variously accuse, vilify, and deny according to their own biases. The people criticize the pastor, and church leaders bemoan the problems of the people in their fellowship. Through all this, the enemy has looked on as Church history has played itself out through the ages, laughing at our inability to stand together for long enough to identify who the enemy actually is and take proper aim in the right direction.

BEATING THE BULLY

Despite the fact that Paul teaches Christians that we are seated in heavenly places with Christ (see Eph. 2:6), it is so easy to abdicate our place next to Him and take up our place with the accuser of the brethren instead (see Rev. 12:10). The problem is that the devil is a bully who will do anything to get a person to give up on his or her faith, marriage, job, career, or hopes and dreams. His accusations are based around our own or other people's inadequacies, as he variously charges us with being worthless, stupid, filthy, broken, unfixable, and beyond help. The problem is he finds it just too easy to get us to agree with him. He accuses us day and night (see Rev. 12:10) without a break. Shame is heaped on us (though we may not always see it as shame) until we get tired of fighting it off.

It is here that a second factor comes into play. A very human response to feeling bad about ourselves is to attempt to shift the focus onto those around us. We judge ourselves by our intentions and other people by their actions. Instead of trying to find a way to help a brother or sister with their issues, we join the accuser of the brethren against them. Of course, we don't see it like that; we think we are merely giving an opinion, not realizing that our subconscious mind is reasoning that if we can show how wrong someone else is, we will look better in comparison. People may not look so hard at me if I'm pointing at you. Added to that, we are generally so fixated on looking at the negative that we don't have eyes to see the things that are changing about ourselves and others, and we lose the opportunity to celebrate God at work.

We judge ourselves by our intentions and other people by their actions.

Jesus' instruction to us to love our neighbor as ourselves brings a new challenge, because as someone once said, if you don't love yourself, God help your neighbor! The direct degree to which we accept ourselves will be the exact amount that we accept our neighbor. Knowing this gives us the opportunity to do some hard thinking! If we want to stop feeling condemned and unworthy, part of the solution has to be in a change of heart. Trying harder to do better just doesn't work. That's behavior modification, which is a change of life without a change of heart and attitude; and it doesn't work. It may last for a month or even for a year, but eventually, unless the heart is changed, we break down under the tremendous pressure of having to keep up an appearance that is only skin-deep.

HOW DOES A HEART CHANGE?

Only God can change a heart. Only the Creator of the heart knows how it works and what it needs. How does a heart change? By believing what God says about you and not what people say or what the accuser says. While it's true that what others have said to us or about us has significantly shaped our lives, the remedy is to make the choices to believe what God says about us. This entails remembering that God didn't send Jesus into the world to condemn it (see John 3:16-17), but to save it. Religion is all about condemnation, but Christianity is about a relationship with Jesus, the One who came to make us like Him. Religion may bring about a change of behavior, but only a relationship can change your heart. Here's a simple check to tell you whether your Christianity is a religion or a relationship; ask yourself this question: Are you living in condemnation toward yourself and others, or is the heart of Jesus your measuring stick?

Notice that never, at any time, did Jesus stand with the accuser of the brethren. Why then, do we, who are His followers, find it so easy to do that?

A relationship with Jesus is not about following the rules of your particular church but about being in heart-to-heart contact with the one who spoke to the Samaritan woman who'd been passed from man to man (see John 4:27), when no one else

would talk with her. He went to dinner with Matthew, the cheating tax
collector (see Matt. 9:9-10), and He
saved the life of the woman caught in
adultery (see John 8:10-11); and all
because He is into salvation rather
than condemnation. Notice that
never, at any time, did Jesus stand
with the accuser of the brethren. Why
then do we, who are His followers,
find it so easy to do that? Overcoming

Are you living in condemnation toward yourself and others, or is the heart of Jesus your measuring stick?

the accuser and distancing ourselves from him is not about our
own ability but about our choices to stand with the only One who
does not condemn us! When Christians get a revelation of that, the
Church will have a far greater capacity for breakthrough, simply
because the heart of Jesus dictates our attitudes, rather than allowing the accuser the right to do it.

Why are you looking in a tomb for someone who is alive?
(Luke 24:5b).

It's too easy, no matter how mature we are in Christ, to default
to a Christianity in which we look for Jesus in a tomb instead of in
our hearts. All we find in the tomb is legalism, rules, and regula-
tions, instead of the life that comes from the One who is Life.

It's Not Who We Are but Whose We Are That Counts (Numbers 22-24)

When the Body of Christ gains revelation on whose we are,
much of our pride, condemnation, and irritation will be dis-
pensed with, allowing us to have God's perspective not just on
ourselves but on His people as a whole.

Here is the story of the people of Israel at a time when they
were preparing to take the Promised Land. For 40 years they had
wandered in wilderness, and now they were parked on the plains

of Moab. It seemed as though they'd been camped there forever, but their next move would be to follow Joshua across the Jordan and into the land God had promised to them. Standing there on the brink of a new season, they were a people prepared and ready for something new, something exciting, something that would require every vestige of faith they had. Those who had lived as slaves were now dead, and this new generation was not bound by the victim mentality of their parents. They were fresh and young and prepared for battle, yet the success of their mission relied not on who they were, but Whose they were.

Camped down there on the plains and engrossed in the activities of their day-to-day living with all its labor, irritation, and boredom, they didn't realize that the very sight of them filled their enemy with terror. Massed together and unaware of onlookers, they had no idea that the Moabite king, Balak, was stricken with fear because of them, and was already gathering allies together to help him conquer them before they conquered him. Knowing through recent history that this people had God on their side, Balak sought spiritual reinforcement in the person of a noted prophet and magician, Balaam—a man who seemed to have power in the spiritual realm and who was able to bring about blessing or cursing on people's lives.

We have that same power today. How we speak about our children and partners, our pastors and churches, our jobs and communities, has great power to affect the outcome of our lives and the lives of others. It is for this reason that anyone who wants to be used by God as one of His catalysts must take great care to speak the language of life rather than death (see Prov. 18:21), because bitterness is contagious and has tremendous power to destroy churches as well as families and friendships (see Heb. 12:15).

Balaam was a curious mixture—a man who was obviously acquainted with God but who didn't feel that God was his only option. Apart from hearing from God, he also worked with enchantments and sacrifices to foreign gods. When the messengers arrived with Balak's summons to come and curse the people, Balaam heard from God immediately. He was instructed not to go with the messengers, nor was he to curse the people God had chosen to bless. He sent the messengers away, even while suffering obvious chagrin over the loss of a good deal of money and kudos...but that wasn't the end of the story. More messengers came who were even more important than the last, and he sought God again. This time God released him to go, but to speak only what he was told to say.

HAVING IT YOUR OWN WAY

There are times when God will give us our own way if we insist on it, but it doesn't mean He is happy with what we are doing. Sometimes it's just that He stops trying to get through to a person who is dazzled by the things he wants, and allows that person to experience the consequences of his desires. It's worthwhile to remember that when He says "no," He means it, but He won't keep saying the same things over and over to people who heard Him the first time. In His Word He has said, "No adultery, no lying, no stealing, no fornicating, no gossiping"; yet often these are the very things we long to do. But "no" means "no" as far as God is concerned. However, Balaam was too foolish, greedy, and proud to realize that. He didn't understand that if you have a disagreement with God and you win...you just lost!

Eventually, the journey itself helped him to see how God felt about him going. But at first, when an angel took a stand against Balaam to bar his way, he didn't see it. This was the man who referred to himself as "the one who sees clearly" (see Num. 24:3), yet he was not able to see the Angel of the Lord standing in his way with a drawn sword, ready to kill him. Even though the prophetic gifting is tightly interwoven with the purposes of God and God doesn't withdraw the gifting once it is given (see Rom. 11:29), it is worth noting that unless the prophet chooses obedience to God's purposes over fame and fortune, it becomes too easy to miss the hand of God in situations that even a donkey can see.

Three times the donkey attempted to stop, but each time the "all-seeing" prophet beat her to make her go on. Finally, God opened her mouth, and she spoke to him in his own language; yet he still didn't catch on. It's amazing how long it takes some of the most gifted people to catch on to the fact that God may be saying "NO!" He resists the proud, but pours out His amazing grace on those who are humble (see 1 Pet. 5:5). He is not the slightest bit interested in our giftings or our great abilities; He's far more interested in the state of our hearts. There are times when He resists us strongly, yet, like Balaam, we are determined that we are right and that God is with us. This is a terrible place to be, because disaster always lies at the end of that road, no matter how beautiful the scenery is. God will not allow us to do in His name what we have decided upon for ourselves, and it is here that taking the name of the Lord in vain takes on a whole new twist (see Deut. 5:11).

Balaam was well aware that he couldn't say anything other than what God said; but when he arrived at Balak's camp, he did not indicate to the king that God was intending to bless His people. He sacrificed a number of animals, perhaps in the hope that God would change His mind (see 1 Sam. 15:22), and then went to check out the view.

Looking down, he saw a portion of God's people and spontaneously began to speak a powerful blessing over them (see Num. 23:7-10), much to Balak's consternation. The amazing thing was that these people were such a quarrelsome rebellious bunch, always complaining about something and often disobedient to

God, yet the view from above showed them to be awesomely beautiful. That's because God's perspective on the people He loves passionately is more easily seen from above.

And God raised us up with Christ and seated us with Him in the heavenly realms in Christ Jesus (Ephesians 2:6 NIV).

The closer you are to Christ when you're looking at the people of God, the more beautiful they become, because you're seeing them from God's perspective.

CHRISTIANS HAVE THEIR FATHER'S EYES

The king was nothing if not persistent, and this time he took Balaam to look at the back end of the people, figuring that the weaker and more feeble strays would be far less appealing to God. At this point, however, God increased the blessing (see Num. 23:13-14,19-21), proving that His love for us does not depend on how well we are doing. By now, less determined individuals would have given up; but despite all the evidence to the contrary, hope continued to beat in Balak's heart, and he found an even better viewpoint with which to give a different perspective. Unfortunately for him, it didn't! In fact, the blessing increased even more, and Balak was furious (see Num. 24:5-10).

The closer you are to Christ when you're looking at the people of God, the more beautiful they become, because you're seeing them from God's perspective.

Balaam's words at this time were so powerful, expressing the passionate love God has for His people, even speaking of the beauty of their homes. You can hear His intention for His people down through the ages. He is determined to bless them, and this story illustrates that it's vital that we do the same, regardless of how it feels when we are up close and personal with the group of people who constitute our church.

As Christians we so often get it wrong. We think our effectiveness depends on ourselves and our abilities, but really, it's not about who we are, but about Whose we are. Our enemy wants to make sure that the Church is seen in the worst possible light. Repeatedly, the king brought the one who was to curse God's people to new heights, feeling sure that if he could just see them from a certain angle, their faults and failures and inadequacies would give enough reason to curse them. Up close and personal, it's not hard to see the failures and the problems of the Church. Even if everything looks okay from one angle, the enemy will make sure we see things from another place, another angle, another perspective so that we are forced to acknowledge the reasonableness of speaking negatively over the Church. In spite of our need at times to stop and pay attention to issues that have been raised in church life, it's vital for the success of the mandate that members guard what they say and don't speak the enemy's language of negativity and bitterness over the people of God.

Regardless of your opinion or mine, the Church is *God's* people, and the emphasis there is not on the people, but on the God to whom they belong. It's not about who we are but about Whose we are. The power is from God through His people. The righteousness is from God on His people. The love is from God, expressed by His people. It's all to do with perspective, and the higher you get in terms of closeness to Christ, the greater your ability to see from God's perspective. Balak thought that taking Balaam higher and higher would help him see the weakness better, when in actual fact the very opposite is true. When we take our seats next to Christ in heavenly places, we will always see from God's perspective. Church life may not always be easy; in fact, it often isn't. But it's vital that we keep God's view as we work through the relevant issues honestly and with love.

When Nehemiah was working day and night with the other laborers to build the walls that would protect the city of God, he found that there was never a shortage of criticism. They came at him in groups, because people usually ridicule and mock in gangs (see Neh. 4:1-3). We learn here that it's important for someone who wants to have a catalytic effect for the Kingdom of God to make the choice to stay away from those who gossip about the Church. Don't live too near the enemy or you will end up speaking his language (see Neh. 4:12).

Leaders in the Church often become weary from the constant pressure of criticism and judgment and the fear that is kindled by listening to what the enemy thinks about the work being done. As God's people, we are called to speak the language of faith, not just over the things we can relate with, but over all the work that God is doing through His Church.

Discouragement is one of the greatest weapons the enemy uses against Christians. Good church people at times find themselves overwhelmed by feelings of rejection and disillusionment because things aren't going right in the church and the people are being damaged. Pastors fall morally or financially sometimes; or they may not understand principles of good leadership; or the difficulties of life have overtaken them, and they lose the will to continue to lead effectively. All this has major implications for the church they lead, often resulting in hurt people who feel as though they have been used up and discarded. Gifted people are left on the shelf while others feel overworked and undervalued. At times the church seems to have lost its vision. And yet in the middle of all this, the Church is still God's answer to the world. Regardless of all the sometimes petty and often tragic problems plaguing the Church, the view from above is still amazing. God sees His people, with all their insecurity and infighting and indifference, as being the Bride of His Son, Jesus Christ. He never gives up on us. He never stands with the accuser over us, and He longs for us to have His perspective, despite the issues we are facing.

Our mandate is to usher in His Kingdom by proclaiming the truth of the Gospel and discipling people and nations after Jesus Christ. Don't waste time listening to an enemy who is terrified of us because he understands Whose we are even more than we do. Don't abandon ship and miss out on the incredible opportunities that being in church will give you to serve the living God and His purposes for the world. There will always be people whose main vision is to criticize and point out all the faults and failings of people who are working hard for the Lord, but those people generally accomplish very little themselves. Not only that, but they are also dangerous friends to have, desiring as they do to infect and infest the Church with a negativity that attempts to demoralize and destroy the work of those whose desire is to usher in the Kingdom.

THEY SAY

Have you heard of the terrible family "They,"
And the dreadful venomous things They say.
Why half the gossip under the sun
If you trace it back, you will find begun
In that wretched house of They.

A numerous family, so I'm told,
And its genealogical tree is old,
For ever since Adam and Eve began
To build up the curious race of man,
Has existed the house of "They."

Gossip mongers and spreaders of lies,
Horrid people whom all despise,
And yet the best of us, now and then,
Repeat queer tales about women and men,
And quote the house of They.

They live like lords and never labor,
They's one task is to watch their neighbor,
And tell his business and private affairs
To the world at large; They are sowers of tares,
These folks of the house of They.

It is wholly useless to follow a They
With a whip or a gun, for he slips away,
And into his house, where you cannot go,
For it's locked and bolted and guarded so,
This horrible house of They.

You cannot get in, yet They get out
And spread their villainous tales about.
Of all the rascals under the sun
Who have come to punishment,
Never one belonged to the house of They.

Author Unknown

Each of us is unique, yet we all are called and appointed for a certain work that only God knows. Our uniqueness is what causes people to minister in ways that others may not understand, approve of, or relate with; but we all march together to the sound of a drumbeat that comes from God. In doing so, we are the Church of Jesus Christ, the multifaceted display of His wisdom to the spiritual world. Like a diamond, the Church variously shows different aspects of the purposes of God; but as a whole, each facet catches the eye, and in doing so, displays the rich beauty of the entire jewel (see Eph. 3:10). Regardless of the problems and difficulties that accompany taking an active part in church life, it's vital that we remember that it is the Church, and only the Church, that is the hope of the world. Don't jump ship...be a part of the solution not the problem.

CHAPTER TEN

The Worth of a Life

Evil is like a shadow—it has no real substance of its own; it is simply a lack of light. You cannot cause a shadow to disappear by trying to fight it, stamp on it, by railing against it, or any other form of emotional or physical resistance. In order to cause a shadow to disappear, you must shine light on it.

Shakti Gawain

WHAT IS A LIFE WORTH?

Have you ever wondered what your life is worth?

The generation alive on the earth today is very confused and messed up over the issue of the worth of a life. On one side, there are millions of lives being flushed out of wombs very easily and cheaply through national health systems across the world every year. On the other hand, millions and millions of dollars are spent annually on IVF and other fertility treatments. People are pouring all the money they can beg, borrow, or steal into their desperation for just one child—a little baby exactly the same as the one who is being tossed away in another hospital bed. I have friends who have spent tens of thousands of dollars to adopt one little girl from China, the place where hundreds of little girls are thrown away every day.

So, what is a life worth? What is life worth to a generation whose brothers and sisters and peers have been aborted because their lives were considered inconvenient? Horrifying and dehumanizing as war is, it is when warfare is internalized into a society by the legitimizing of the killing of its own young that confusion over the value of life becomes intrinsically fixed into the psyche of the nation.

So, what is a life worth? Does it depend on whose life it is? Is the life of a princess or a rock star of more value than the life of your neighbor or someone with Downe's Syndrome? Was Mother Theresa's life more valuable than the life of someone you don't like? Furthermore, does the value we give to our own life pivot around the answers to these questions?

ONE SOLITARY LIFE

He was born in an obscure village, the child of a peasant woman. He grew up in another village where he worked in a carpenter's shop until he was thirty. Then, for three years he was an itinerant preacher. He never wrote a book. He never held an office. He never traveled more than two hundred miles from the place where he was born. He did none of the things one usually associates with greatness. He was only thirty-three when the tide of public opinion turned against him. He was turned over to his enemies and went through the mockery of a trial. He was

nailed to a cross between two thieves. When he was dead,
he was laid in a borrowed grave. Twenty centuries have
come and gone and today he is the central figure of the
human race and leader of mankind's progress. All the
armies that ever marched, all the navies that ever sailed,
all the kings that ever reigned have not affected the life of
man as much as that One Solitary Life...
Jesus Christ of Nazareth.

Author Unknown

Jesus led an incredibly valuable life. He redeemed us, cleansed us, influenced us, and has given us a reason to live. It's as we live our lives in Him and through Him that we will not only gain perspective of the value of our life, but also the value of the lives of those around us.

John the Baptist, when faced with the understanding that the One whose arrival he had been announcing had now come, said, *"He must increase, but I must decrease"* (John 3:30 KJV). This is a useful prayer for us to pray when we are struggling with the desire to increase ourselves, which means that He decreases in us. This conflict happens regularly in me. My own opinions and desires struggle to increase in my heart, and the only way I can break the cycle of self that sets itself up yet again is to come back to Jesus Christ to ask again that He would increase in me. The only way for my life to be effective is for Him to increase in me and for me to decrease in myself.

The only way for my life to be effective is for Him to increase in me and for me to decrease in myself.

For whoever wants to save his life will lose it, but whoever loses his life for Me will save it (Luke 9:24 NIV).

One way or another we will lose our life; therefore, it's vital that we lose it for the right reasons. He alone is the One who enables us to lose it for a purpose.

So, what is a life worth? It depends on the perspective you're viewing from. Unless we have already settled the issue of the worth of a life in our hearts according to Jesus' measure, we will always unconsciously sum up each person we meet, and our evaluation of them will always be according to our own prejudices and values. Therefore, the life of the prostitute will always weigh less when we hear of her murder, than the life of a young girl who just brilliantly completed her senior school exams. The life of 4,000 people in the New York towers, a people group we can identify with, will weigh more than double or triple the value of the same number of people whose culture we can't identify with in Afghanistan, despite the fact that they have been living in fear of those same terrorists for years. Unless we have settled the issue of once-and-for-all in our hearts, we will always judge the value of a life from our own value system, which directly relates with what we are familiar with.

ONE LIFE FOR MANY

For God so loved the world...so valued the world...that He gave (see John 3:16). What did He give? He gave a life—one life in exchange for lives—billions of lives. One life for many! So what's the worth of a life? The life of Jesus had enough weight on the heavenly scales to buy the life of every person who has ever lived. However, incredibly, every individual person who has ever lived has enough weight alone on those same scales to be worth the life of the Son of God. That's bizarre!

What's the worth of a life? It depends on who's asking.

THE UNINVITED GUEST—DANIEL 5

Here is the story of a king who was having a party. Belshazzar felt his life was worth a great deal. He'd never been denied anything and felt that he deserved to have whatever he wanted, which caused him to make a terrible mistake. His decision to use the gold and silver cups that had been stolen by the Babylonians from the temple for his party guests to drink from was a bad one. The wine flowed, and everyone was getting drunk as they swilled the wine from the cups that had been dedicated to God. But then God showed up at that party to weigh the worth of the king's life. Suddenly and gruesomely, a hand appeared on the wall and began to write what amounted to be the details of Belshazzar's life (see Dan. 5:25-28). *Numbered...numbered...weighed...divided*—the king's life was summed up in terms of what God had created him to be and do, and there now was the evaluation for all to see. In terms of what Belshazzar was created for and equipped to do (see Eph. 2:10), his life was worth nothing. He had wasted it!

Our worth to God is set in that Jesus died for each one of us individually. There's nothing we can do to earn our salvation; it has been given to us because of His love alone and not because of our excellence. Our worth in effectiveness, however, is completely different. The worth of a life in effectiveness is displayed in direct proportion to our willingness to lay it down, that is, to lose it, or to put it more clearly, to let God have His way with it.

WHAT'S MY LIFE WORTH?

So, what's a life worth? To bring it more close to home, ask yourself the question: What's *my* life worth? In recent years, I've had to ask that question of myself repeatedly at deeper and deeper levels. Hurts, disappointments, and the dreadful feeling of failure caused severe loss of confidence in myself and my ministry, making me question whether I even had what it took to be effective for God. I had to examine every aspect of who I am as a person, as a leader in the church, why I am in ministry, what my motivations are, and whether what I do is really of any use to God. The underscore of the decision I needed to make as to whether to stay in ministry or get out was based around biblical principles. One of these related to the words of Jesus to His disciples concerning the fruit they were to bear. Was my fruit of any value, or could it be easily spoiled, disappearing not long after it appeared?

> *You did not choose Me, but I chose you and appointed you that you should go and bear fruit, and that your fruit should remain* (John 15:16a NKJV).

In addition to that, my internal questioning revolved around who was doing the building of the ministry I was called to—God or me? It is so easy to lose perspective on what and who all our activity is actually for and begin to expend feverish energy on something that isn't worth anything anyway.

> *Unless the Lord builds the house, they labor in vain who build it* (Psalm 127:1a NKJV).

I needed to thoroughly examine myself as I asked these questions. Was I laboring along with God to build His house, or had my call to serve God become my career path, my security, and my picture of myself that needed to be preserved at all costs? Many people in ministry have been aware that the time has come to let go and allow God to bring in someone new with a fresh vision; but fear of losing their salary, their pension, their house, or their honored role has caused them to make the decision to stay longer than they should have, even though God was calling them to a new thing. When this happens, everyone loses out. The Church loses, the ministry loses, but so does the one who chooses not to go on to the next thing God is calling them to. Following God is the most exciting, fulfilling, and scary undertaking a person can take. When a new season begins, you never know where it will take you; but if you know the faithfulness of the One who is calling, you don't have to be afraid. He's going to do what He says He will do (see 1 Thess. 5:24). On a regular basis, we need to ask ourselves the question: Does the ministry I'm laboring so hard in still belong to God, or is it time to allow Him to replace me so the ministry He enabled me to build can live and breathe in a new dimension, and I

The worth of a life in effectiveness is displayed in direct proportion to our willingness to lay it down, that is, to lose it, or to put it more clearly, to let God have His way with it.

can go onto the new season? If we make the choice to stop where we are instead of go on in the journey, we waste precious time that God could be using.

THE CURRENCY OF LIFE

The years and months we live on this earth are currency that has been given to us by God, like dollars to be spent as we choose. When my children were small, their grandmother would sometimes give them money for their birthday. To them it was always a huge sum, and we would encourage them to put the money in a safe place and save it until they found something they really wanted to buy. However, as we all know, it was just so easy to use a little of that money to buy candy and sweets in the afternoon on the way home from school, and a little more to do the same thing when friends come around and wanted to go to the store. Pretty soon, when that fantastic new yo-yo hit the market, or a special school excursion took place, the recipients of the money found they had little or nothing left to buy what they really wanted. It was all spent in small amounts on things that

The years and months we live on this earth are currency that has been given to us by God, like dollars to be spent as we choose.

weren't really important, and they hadn't realized the degree to which they were wasting their money until it was too late.

People do the same thing with the days of their lives; they spend them on stuff that doesn't last and really doesn't matter. And then one day, when they begin to realize the importance of living for God, they find they don't have enough time or energy or money to do what they could have done years before. Don't spend your years on stuff that doesn't last.

> *Do not store up for yourselves treasures on earth, where moth and rust destroy, and where thieves break in and steal. But store up for yourselves treasures in heaven, where moth and rust do not destroy, and where thieves do not break in and steal. For where your treasure is, there your heart will be also* (Matthew 6:19-20 NIV).

WHAT'S TO STOP YOU?

What might keep you from spending the days of your life on the purposes of God? What would stop your life from reaching the maximum in God's purposes?

Drivenness

This is desperately destructive because so often our drivenness relates directly to our ministry call. The supercharged pressures of being the man or woman of faith and power for the hour have the capacity to destroy any ministry. Moses is a great example of this as he sat in his tent from daylight to dark trying to be the best leader he could be and killing himself in the process (see Exod. 18:13-26). It took a word of wisdom from his father-in-law to help him realize that God had more strings to His bow than little old Moses. Many of us don't realize this until it's too late. We use up our time and energy on the urgent needs of the ministry, never realizing the degree to which our family, our health, and our sanity depend on protecting ourselves from extremes of activity. We often lose context of the valuable things we are called to because we are driven by the tyranny of the urgent call to use ourselves up on things that can't seem to manage without us.

Fear of Failure

Remember the story of the talent the servant buried because he was afraid of his master (see Matt. 25:24-26). It wasn't strictly his master he was afraid of; rather, it was failing that he feared and of what his master would do when that happened, which he was sure it would. Most of the disobedience, laziness, and passivity of the Body of Christ ultimately find its roots in the fear of failure. We have such intolerance of mistakes in others that we render ourselves useless through fear of their judgments if we were to make a mistake ourselves, but the problem is that the person who doesn't make a mistake doesn't make anything at all. We are a lot more rigid with our own idea of what God thinks than He is. He's actually very tolerant of our stumbling attempts to do what He asks of us; it's the blatant choices we make to do nothing that gets us into trouble.

Self-determination

Even though Saul had been appointed as king by God, he was determined to rule the people in his own way. God can call a man or woman into ministry and they begin in the same way as Saul did, with a humble heart that is so astonished at the way God has elevated them that they look for a place to hide (see 1 Sam. 10:21-22). It's vital that we don't then do as Saul did—losing his way because he was sure that his own leadership exempted him from doing

God's work God's way. A friend of mine used to preach a great message based on the Australian beach lifesaving system, relating that to the need of living your Christian life within the flags. We can never live outside the flags that God has set up for our safety without ending up losing the destiny He called us to. No one, regardless of their gifts or position in the Body of Christ, is exempt from doing it God's way.

So…what's a life worth? What is your life worth to the purposes of God?

LIVING THE PLAN

Regardless of the style of Christianity you prefer, none of us can fail to admire Mother Theresa and the work she did to represent Jesus Christ among the poorest people in India. What most people don't know is that she wasn't always a tiny, wizened up, old nun. Once she was a beautiful, funny, Princess Charming who had the world at her feet. The dearly loved and cosseted daughter of a wealthy Albanian family, she was rich and highly sought after…what was her life worth at that stage?

Yet she gave it all away for something of greater value—the plan of God. She gave up her life of leisure, pleasure, and treasure to live out her destiny. She left behind the plan her parents had; she refused the plan her friends had; she even let go of all her own plans because she had a revelation of what it is to live for God.

> *"For I know the plans I have for you," says the Lord. "They are plans for good and not for disaster, to give you a future and a hope"* (Jeremiah 29:11).

Mother Theresa identified with Paul when he said that if anyone thought they had a reason to think they were okay, it was him (see Phil. 3:4-14). He was a Pharisee with all the trimmings, and the trajectory of his career path appeared to be taking him to the position of high priest; yet he said he realized it was all garbage in comparison to knowing Jesus Christ and living for Him alone.

In the same way, Mother Theresa gave up everything her family held dear, everything her friends envied her, and every comfort that she might otherwise experience so that she could know Jesus and His surpassing greatness. She made the decision to spend her life on something of value. And what was the currency of her life buying? It was buying people!

> *Since you are precious and honored in My sight, and because I love you, I will give men in exchange for you, and people in exchange for your life* (Isaiah 43:4 NIV).

What will you get if you lay down your life in the service of Jesus Christ? What will the currency of your days and months and years buy? They will buy people for the Kingdom of God…maybe a handful, maybe a community, maybe a nation of people. We will never know the effect our lives could have if we let Jesus have His way unless we do it. In the Scripture above, the word "men" in the Hebrew is *adam*, which means "mankind; human beings." The word "people" translates as "community; nation; a people group."

God paid for the currency of Mother Theresa's years with an astonishing purchase—a nation of people. He exchanged her life for desperately poor people and desperate rich people, with dignitaries and sick people, with children and with old people. He paid in the same kind for Billy Graham's life and Gladys Aylward's life, for John Wesley's and Lord Shaftsbury's and Harriet Tubman's lives; and He will pay in the same way for your life too, if you make the ongoing choices to let Him. What might happen in your street or your workplace or community or nation if you begin to take this Scripture literally? How might God pay for your life, and with whom?

WHERE THE RUBBER HITS THE ROAD

What's your life worth?

The answer to that is another question: To whom? You see, it depends on who is asking. If it's God asking, then the answer ties in with His mandate to go into all the world and preach the Gospel, making disciples of nations. Jesus gave up His life as a ransom for us; it was a payment that freed many people. And He gives us the privilege of giving our lives to the same cause. He's never in debt to anyone; He will pay for the use of our lives with people—peers, people we have not yet met, children—ours and other people's, men and women whose heart's desire is for something more, but who need a catalyst to help them grasp the purposes of God for themselves. You can be that catalyst, if you will allow yourself to see yourself as God sees you and place the same value on your life as He does. He will give men for your life, and people in exchange for your life.

So, how much is your life worth? Well, spent on yourself, it's worth only what you can manage to touch and hold for yourself, and the fruit that is borne is quickly used up. But, in terms of effectiveness, when a person gives his life to God wholly, without drivenness to please Him, or the paralyzing fear of failing Him, or determination to serve Him in his own way; when a person gives his life to God saying, "It's Yours, Lord. I will no longer choose my own way but will trust You to lead me into Your plan for my life," then, on those eternal scales that only God can understand, a miracle begins to take place. *Numbered, numbered, weighed*…what's there on the other half of the scale? Children, men, women, people groups, even nations may be there. Who can guess what a life can be worth…when it's given to God?

The amazing thing about God is that He will do in and with us things we never would have done or thought of doing and no one else would have ever thought of those things either. Your destiny in God and the life you would choose for yourself have almost nothing in common. This is not about the difference between being a Christian or not; this is about the degree to which you are surrendered to His plan for your life. You may live a good Christian life with a great church attendance record; you may have a fine ministry and give away lots of

> *Revivals don't change people; they throw up people who give their life to Christ so that the world will be changed.*
>
> Gerald Coates

money, yet so much of what we do for God is dictated by our fear of failure, our drivenness, and our determination to do it our way. God can do more in a life given over to Him than we could possibly imagine in our wildest dreams. Gerald Coates said, "Revivals don't change people; they throw up people who give their life to Christ so that the world will be changed." Is that you? Are you the one who is prepared to lay down your life and allow God to use it as currency to exchange for other human beings...even for other nations?

Even though giving up your life for the purposes of God is the hardest thing a person can do, it is also not that difficult. Once you get in the habit of saying "yes" to God, it becomes easier and easier. It entails absorbing the revelation that life is more than the 70 to 100 years we may have on this earth, if we're fortunate. Once we understand that, the decision about how we spend those years becomes simple. In light of eternity, those years are nothing, yet they are all the time we have in which to make the decision. Once the decision is made and we begin to live that way in truth, we then begin to see what God intends for us and marvel at how close we came to letting our littleness of comprehension and tiny perspective almost get in the way of an awesome life.

What's a life worth?

What's your life worth?

The whole thing pivots on His feelings for us; His love for us is so pure and strong and clean that He sees us as precious, regardless of how we see ourselves. He honors us by allowing us to work alongside Him in establishing the Kingdom of God, and when we make the choice to do it, He overwhelms us by paying for the use of our life by bringing people in from every walk of life—skaters, businesspeople, young wives, old men, drug addicts, abused, privileged, AIDs victims. The categories of people groups are endless, and you are called to go to at least one of them to show them how much Jesus loves them.

Since you are precious and honored in My sight, and because I love you, I will give men in exchange for you, and people in exchange for your life.

Isaiah 43:4 NIV

Give your life and times to God again; they will increase in value as you do so, as He works together with you to change your world. There's no greater privilege than serving as a catalyst to usher in the Kingdom of Heaven on earth. Astonish yourself by letting Him use you to change your world.

CONTACT THE AUTHOR

Bev Murrill
Christian Growth International
Chelmsford, Essex, UK

E-mail:
bev@christiangrowthinternational.org

How to Equip Believers in the Revelatory Realm of Dreams and Visions

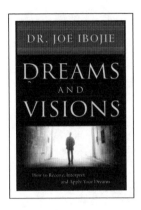

DREAMS AND VISIONS

How To Receive, Interpret and Apply Your Dreams

BY DR. JOE IBOJIE

Dreams and Visions presents sound scriptural principles and practical instructions to help us understand dreams and visions. It seeks to equip believers in the revelatory realm of dreams, their interpretation and usefulness in our everyday living.

The book provides readers with the necessary understanding to approach dreams and visions by the Holy Spirit, through biblical illustrations, understanding of the meaning of dreams and prophetic symbolism, and by exploring the art of dream interpretation according to ancient methods of the Bible.

ISBN 13: 978-88-89127-13-1

Order Now from Destiny Image Europe
Telephone: +39 085 4716623 - Fax +39 085 4716622
E-mail: ordini@eurodestinyimage.com

Internet: www.eurodestinyimage.com

A new exciting title from
DESTINY IMAGE EUROPE

PATHWAYS TO DESTINY

Understanding Your Journey Toward True Purpose in Life

BY SHEENA RYAN

Are your dreams still waiting to be fulfilled?

God has set pathways before you especially designed to lead you into your destiny. You might have wondered why you seem to walk round and round in circles, never quite entering into God's promises for your life.

Pathways to Destiny shines light upon the pathways that everyone needs to successfully negotiate, so that their destiny will become a present experience instead of a distant hope.

This might well be the most important book you read this year!

ISBN 13: 978-88-89127-42-1

Order Now from Destiny Image Europe
Telephone: +39 085 4716623 - Fax +39 085 4716622
E-mail: ordini@eurodestinyimage.com

Internet: www.eurodestinyimage.com

Additional copies of this book and other book
titles from DESTINY IMAGE EUROPE
are available at your local bookstore.

We are adding new titles every month!

To view our complete catalog on-line, visit us at:
www.eurodestinyimage.com

Send a request for a catalog to:

**Via Acquacorrente, 6
65123 - Pescara - ITALY
Tel. +39 085 4716623 - Fax +39 085 4716622**

"Changing the world, one book at a time."

Are you an author?

Do you have a "today" God-given message?

CONTACT US

We will be happy to review your manuscript
for a possible publishing:

publisher@eurodestinyimage.com